ASSESSMENT

MW00955082

On Core
Mathematics

Grade 2

HOUGHTON MIFFLIN HARCOURT

Cover photo credit: Garry Gay/Alamy

Printed in the U.S.A.

ISBN 978-0-547-59046-2

 5 6 7 8 9 10 2266 20 19 18 17 16 15 14 13

4500451729   ^ B C D E F G

Table of Contents

Operations and Algebraic Thinking

Number and Operations in Base Ten

▶ **Understand place value.**

▶ Use place value understanding and properties of operations to add and subtract.

Measurement and Data

▶ **Represent and interpret data.**

Geometry

▶ **Reason with shapes and their attributes.**

Geometry

1. Eli has 13 marbles. Amber has 6 marbles. How many more marbles does Eli have than Amber?

13

6	

○ 7
○ 8
○ 10
○ 19

2. There were 8 ants on a rock. Some more ants joined them. Then there were 13 ants on the rock. How many ants joined them?

○ 4
○ 5
○ 13
○ 22

3. Julian has 14 grapes. He gives 5 grapes to Lindsay. How many grapes does Julian have left?

	5

14

○ 19
○ 11
○ 10
○ 9

4. Sarah had 6 books. Her grandmother gave her 5 more books. How many books does Sarah have now?

○ 1
○ 10
○ 11
○ 13

5. Jared has 15 red cubes. He has 7 blue cubes. How many more red cubes than blue cubes does he have? Complete the bar model.

15

7	

_____ more red cubes

_____

Operations and Algebraic Thinking

1. There are 14 bees in an apple tree. There are 9 bees in a pear tree. How many more bees are in the apple tree than in the pear tree?

Which number sentence could you use to solve the problem?

○ $9 + 14 = $ ▢

○ ▢ $ + 9 = 14$

○ $9 = $ ▢ $ + 14$

○ $14 = 9 - $ ▢

2. There are 11 children at the park. Then 5 children go home. Which number sentence shows how many children are still at the park?

○ $8 - 4 = 4$

○ $11 - 5 = 6$

○ $11 + 5 = 16$

○ $11 + 6 = 17$

3. Lenny had 16 toy cars. He gave some cars to his sister. Now he has 9 cars. Which number sentence shows how many cars he gave to his sister?

○ $16 - 9 = 7$

○ $9 - 2 = 7$

○ $16 - 6 = 10$

○ $16 + 2 = 18$

4. Write a number sentence for the problem. Use a ▢ for the missing number. Then solve.

Ann read 4 pages of a book. Then she read 8 more pages. How many pages did she read altogether?

_____

_____ **pages**

© Houghton Mifflin Harcourt Publishing Company

1. James and Flora have 38 markers in all. Flora has 16 markers. How many markers does James have?

   ○ 22   ○ 54
   ○ 44   ○ 62

2. A pet store has two fish tanks. There are 48 fish in one tank and 23 fish in the other tank. How many fish are there in both tanks?

   ○ 25   ○ 71
   ○ 26   ○ 72

3. Miles puts 52 stickers in his notebook. Julie puts 29 stickers in her notebook. How many stickers do Miles and Julie put in their notebook in all?

   ○ 23   ○ 81
   ○ 71   ○ 94

4. There are 37 pencils in the pencil box. Ms. Marks hands out 18 of the pencils to the class. How many pencils are left in the pencil box?

   ○ 55   ○ 25
   ○ 29   ○ 19

5. Label the bar model. Write a number sentence with a ▨ for the missing number. Solve.

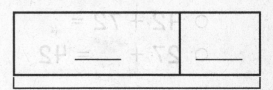

   Tom has 23 red pens and 38 black pens how man pens does Tom have?

   _____

   _____ pens

1. Gina scores 26 points in the game. Eric scores 31 points. Which number sentence can be used to find how many they score in all?

   ○ $26 + \blacksquare = 31$
   ○ $31 + \blacksquare = 55$
   ○ $26 + 31 = \blacksquare$
   ○ $31 + 62 = \blacksquare$

3. Tim and Liz collect stamps. Tim has 93 stamps. Liz has 32 stamps. How many stamps do Tim and Liz have in all?

   ○ 125   ○ 115
   ○ 120   ○ 105

2. On a hike, Sierra sees 42 frogs and 27 turtles. Which number sentence can be used to find how many frogs and turtles Sierra sees in all?

   ○ $\blacksquare + 24 = 27$
   ○ $42 + 27 = \blacksquare$
   ○ $42 + 72 = \blacksquare$
   ○ $27 + \blacksquare = 42$

4. Amber collects 49 pebbles at the beach. Meg collects 44 pebbles at the beach. How many pebbles do they collect in all?

   ○ 103
   ○ 93
   ○ 83
   ○ 5

5. Write a number sentence for the problem. Use a $\blacksquare$ for the missing number. Then solve.

   63 people ride on the bus. 37 of them are adults and the rest are children. How many children are on the bus?

   _____

   _____ children

© Houghton Mifflin Harcourt Publishing Company

1. Mrs. Dobbs has 38 stickers. She gives away 12 stickers. Which number sentence shows how many stickers she has left?

```
┌──────────┬──────────┐
│  ____    │   ____   │
└──────────┴──────────┘
      ____
```

- ○ 26 − 12 = 14
- ○ 12 + 26 = 38
- ○ 38 − 12 = 26
- ○ 12 − 6 = 6

3. Alison makes 54 cookies. She gives away 32 cookies. Which number sentence shows how many cookies she has left?

```
┌──────────┬──────────┐
│  ____    │   ____   │
└──────────┴──────────┘
      ____
```

- ○ 54 + 32 = 86
- ○ 32 + 50 = 82
- ○ 32 − 12 = 20
- ○ 54 − 32 = 22

2. Which bar model shows the number sentence?

$$22 - 8 = 14$$

○
```
┌──────────┬──────┐
│    14    │   8  │
└──────────┴──────┘
       14
```

○
```
┌──────────┬──────┐
│    14    │   8  │
└──────────┴──────┘
       22
```

○
```
┌────────┬────────┐
│   22   │   14   │
└────────┴────────┘
        8
```

○
```
┌────────┬──────┐
│   22   │   8  │
└────────┴──────┘
       14
```

4. Larry had 46 carrots. Rabbits ate 27 carrots. How many carrots does he have left? Label the bar model. Write a number sentence with a 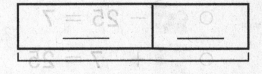 for the missing number. Solve.

```
┌──────────┬──────────┐
│  ____    │   ____   │
└──────────┴──────────┘
```

_____

_____

1. There were 27 children in a classroom. Then 18 children went outside. Which number sentence can be used to find how many children are in the classroom now?

   ○ $27 + 18 =$ ▮

   ○ $18 - 27 =$ ▮

   ○ $45 - 27 =$ ▮

   ○ $27 - 18 =$ ▮

2. Ms. Clark baked some cookies. She gave 25 cookies to her friends. Now she has 7 cookies. Which number sentence can be used to find how many cookies she baked?

   ○ ▮ $+ 25 = 7$

   ○ ▮ $- 25 = 7$

   ○ ▮ $+ 7 = 25$

   ○ ▮ $- 25 = 32$

3. Tom had 45 marbles. He gave 31 marbles to his sister. Which number sentence can be used to find how many marbles Tom has now?

   ○ $45 - 31 =$ ▮

   ○ $31 - 45 =$ ▮

   ○ $45 + 31 =$ ▮

   ○ $76 - 31 =$ ▮

4. There were 36 apples on a tree. Some apples fell down. Now there are 11 apples on the tree. Which number sentence can be used to find how many apples fell down?

   ○ $36 +$ ▮ $= 11$

   ○ $11 -$ ▮ $= 36$

   ○ $36 -$ ▮ $= 11$

   ○ $25 -$ ▮ $= 11$

5. Write a problem for the number sentence
   $30 -$ ▮ $= 14.$

   _____

   _____

Operations and Algebraic Thinking

1. There were 53 people in line at the movies. Then 17 people left the line. Later, 22 more people left. How many people are in line now?

   ○ 4   ○ 24
   ○ 14   ○ 58

2. Molly has 39 coins in her collection. Her sister has 26 coins. How many more coins are needed so they will have 85 coins in all?

   ○ 20   ○ 30
   ○ 21   ○ 65

3. Jack counted 48 ants on one log and 33 ants on another log. Some ants left. Then there were 54 ants in all. How many ants left?

   ○ 17   ○ 27
   ○ 21   ○ 81

4. There were 24 ducks on a pond. Then 27 more ducks came to the pond. Later, 14 ducks flew away. How many ducks are on the pond now?

   ○ 51   ○ 27
   ○ 37   ○ 21

5. Mr. Lane drove 42 miles. Then he drove 35 miles. He plans to drive 87 miles in all. How much farther does he need to drive? Draw bar models to help you solve the problem.

_____ miles

Operations and Algebraic Thinking

1. Which doubles fact could you use to find the sum?

$4 + 5 =$ _____

- ○ $3 + 3 = 6$
- ○ $4 + 6 = 10$
- ○ $5 + 5 = 10$
- ○ $6 + 6 = 12$

2. Which doubles fact could you use to find the sum?

$9 + 8 =$ _____

- ○ $8 + 8 = 16$
- ○ $7 + 7 = 14$
- ○ $9 + 1 = 10$
- ○ $10 + 10 = 20$

3. What is the sum?

$7 + 6 =$ _____

- ○ 11
- ○ 12
- ○ 13
- ○ 14

4. Maggie picked 3 apples. Lisa picked 4 apples. How many apples did they pick in all?

- ○ 6
- ○ 7
- ○ 8
- ○ 9

5. Kevin has 5 marbles. Jen has 6 marbles. How many marbles do they have in all?

Write a doubles fact you can use to find the sum.
Then write the sum.

_____

_____

_____

1. What is the sum for both number sentences?

   $6 + 1 =$ _____

   $1 + 6 =$ _____

   ○ 4
   ○ 5
   ○ 6
   ○ 7

2. What is the sum?

   $8 + 7 =$ _____

   ○ 13
   ○ 14
   ○ 15
   ○ 16

3. Which of the following has the same sum?

   $2 + 9 = ?$

   ○ $8 + 2$
   ○ $9 + 2$
   ○ $2 + 10$
   ○ $3 + 9$

4. Marco had 6 stamps. His mother gave him 3 more stamps. How many stamps does Marco have now?

   ○ 7
   ○ 8
   ○ 9
   ○ 10

5. Explain why $5 + 4$ and $4 + 5$ have the same sum.

   _____

   _____

   _____

Operations and Algebraic Thinking

1. How could you break apart the 7 to make a ten?

$$6 + 7$$

$$6 + \underline{\hspace{1cm}} + \underline{\hspace{1cm}}$$

- ○ 2 + 5
- ○ 4 + 3
- ○ 5 + 2
- ○ 1 + 6

3. How could you break apart the 9 to make a ten?

$$8 + 9$$

$$8 + \underline{\hspace{1cm}} + \underline{\hspace{1cm}}$$

- ○ 7 + 2
- ○ 4 + 5
- ○ 2 + 7
- ○ 3 + 6

2. What is the sum?

$$9 + 5 = \underline{\hspace{1cm}}$$

- ○ 11
- ○ 12
- ○ 13
- ○ 14

4. What is the sum?

$$4 + 8 = \underline{\hspace{1cm}}$$

- ○ 2
- ○ 12
- ○ 13
- ○ 16

5. Draw to show how you can make a ten to find the sum. Write the sum.

_____

_____

$$5 + 7 = \underline{\hspace{1cm}}$$

$$10 + \underline{\hspace{1cm}} = \underline{\hspace{1cm}}$$

Operations and Algebraic Thinking

1. What is the sum?

$$2 + 4 + 8 = \underline{\hspace{2cm}}$$

- ○ 12
- ○ 14
- ○ 15
- ○ 16

3. What is the sum?

$$
\begin{array}{r}
4 \\
5 \\
+ \ 7 \\
\hline
\end{array}
$$

- ○ 9
- ○ 11
- ○ 16
- ○ 17

2. What is the sum?

$$
\begin{array}{r}
4 \\
3 \\
+ \ 6 \\
\hline
\end{array}
$$

- ○ 13
- ○ 10
- ○ 9
- ○ 7

4. Ava grows 3 red flowers, 4 yellow flowers, and 4 purple flowers in her garden. How many flowers does Ava grow in all?

- ○ 7
- ○ 8
- ○ 10
- ○ 11

5. Solve two ways. Circle the two addends you add first.

$$3 + 7 + 5 = \underline{\hspace{2cm}} \qquad 3 + 7 + 5 = \underline{\hspace{2cm}}$$

Operations and Algebraic Thinking

1. What is the difference for the related subtraction fact?

$$9 + 6 = 15$$

$$15 - 9 = \underline{\hspace{2cm}}$$

○ 3
○ 4
○ 5
○ 6

3. Which shows a related addition fact?

$$13 - 6 = 7$$

○ $6 + 7 = 13$
○ $7 + 13 = 20$
○ $7 - 6 = 1$
○ $13 + 6 = 19$

2. What is the sum for the related addition fact?

$$12 - 7 = 5$$

$$5 + 7 = \underline{\hspace{2cm}}$$

○ 11
○ 12
○ 13
○ 14

4. There are 11 brown birds and 5 red birds in a tree. How many more brown birds than red birds are there?

○ 5
○ 6
○ 7
○ 9

5. Write the sum and the difference for the related facts.

$$8 + 8 = \underline{\hspace{2cm}}$$

$$16 - 8 = \underline{\hspace{2cm}}$$

Operations and Algebraic Thinking

© Houghton Mifflin Harcourt Publishing Company

1. What is the difference?

$$15 - 7 = \underline{\hspace{2cm}}$$

- ○ 7
- ○ 8
- ○ 12
- ○ 15

2. What is the difference?

$$\underline{\hspace{2cm}} = 13 - 9$$

- ○ 4
- ○ 5
- ○ 6
- ○ 7

3. What is the difference?

$$16 - 7 = \underline{\hspace{2cm}}$$

- ○ 9
- ○ 8
- ○ 7
- ○ 6

4. Elena invited 8 friends to her party. 2 of them could not go. How many friends went to Elena's party?

- ○ 2
- ○ 4
- ○ 5
- ○ 6

5. Write the difference.
Draw to show your work.

$$\underline{\hspace{2cm}} = 9 - 4$$

1. Which tens fact could you use to find the difference?

$$11 - 4 = \underline{\hspace{1.5cm}}$$

? ?

- ○ $10 - 5 = 5$
- ○ $10 - 4 = 6$
- ○ $10 - 3 = 7$
- ○ $10 - 2 = 8$

2. Which tens fact could you use to find the difference?

$$16 - 7 = \underline{\hspace{1.5cm}}$$

? ?

- ○ $10 - 4 = 6$
- ○ $10 - 3 = 7$
- ○ $10 - 2 = 8$
- ○ $10 - 1 = 9$

3. Mr. Brown picked 12 plums. He gave 8 plums away. How many plums did he have left?

- ○ 3
- ○ 4
- ○ 5
- ○ 6

4. Which number makes the number sentence true?

$$13 - 5 = 8$$

$$10 - \underline{\hspace{1.5cm}} = 8$$

- ○ 2
- ○ 3
- ○ 4
- ○ 6

5. Show the tens fact you used. Write the difference.

$$12 - 4 = \underline{\hspace{1.5cm}}$$

_____ _____

$$10 - \underline{\hspace{1.5cm}} = \underline{\hspace{1.5cm}}$$

Operations and Algebraic Thinking

© Houghton Mifflin Harcourt Publishing Company

1. The Morris family has an even number of dogs and an odd number of cats. Which could be the number of pets in the Morris family?

   ○ 1 dog and 2 cats
   ○ 1 dog and 3 cats
   ○ 2 dogs and 2 cats
   ○ 2 dogs and 1 cat

2. Elsa shades a pair of ten frames to show an even number. Which could be Elsa's ten frames?

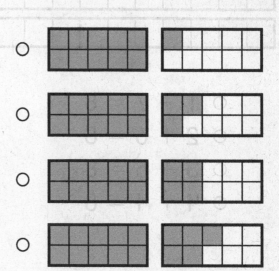

3. Shade this pair of ten frames to show an even number greater than 15. Explain how you know the number is even.

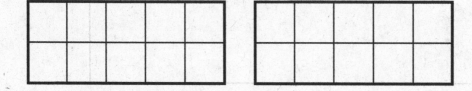

_____

_____

_____

1. The frames show two groups for 8. Which addition sentence shows the groups?

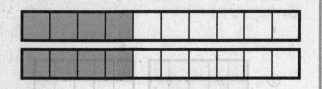

- ○ 1 + 7 = 8
- ○ 2 + 6 = 8
- ○ 3 + 5 = 8
- ○ 4 + 4 = 8

2. Mary and Ana each have the same number of stickers. They have 10 stickers altogether. Which addition sentence shows the number of stickers Mary and Ana each have?

- ○ 4 + 6 = 10
- ○ 5 + 5 = 10
- ○ 3 + 7 = 10
- ○ 2 + 8 = 10

3. Draw to show that 12 is an even number.

1. Ms. Green put 4 stamps on each card. How many stamps will she put on 5 cards?

   ○ 20
   ○ 16
   ○ 9
   ○ 8

2. Gina has 4 mice cages. There are 4 mice in each cage. How many mice does Gina have?

   ○ 8
   ○ 10
   ○ 12
   ○ 16

3. Eric puts his dimes in 5 rows. He puts 3 dimes in each row. How many dimes does he have in all?

   ○ 5
   ○ 8
   ○ 12
   ○ 15

4. Rachel puts 4 pencils in each box. How many pencils will she put in 3 boxes?

   ○ 16
   ○ 12
   ○ 7
   ○ 4

5. Rob puts 3 counters in each row. How many counters in all does he put in 4 rows? Draw to show your work.

_____ counters

1. Which could you use to find the number of squares?

- ○ 5 + 5 + 5 + 5 = ____
- ○ 5 + 5 + 5 = ____
- ○ 4 + 4 + 4 = ____
- ○ 4 + 4 + 4 + 4 = ____

3. Which could you use to find the number of circles?

- ○ 3 + 3 + 3 = ____
- ○ 3 + 3 + 3 + 3 = ____
- ○ 5 + 5 + 5 = ____
- ○ 5 + 5 + 5 + 5 = ____

2. Some children sat in 2 rows. There were 3 children in each row. How many children were there in all?

- ○ 1
- ○ 2
- ○ 5
- ○ 6

4. Mr. Henry has 4 rows of trees. There are 2 trees in each row. How many trees does he have in all?

- ○ 10
- ○ 8
- ○ 6
- ○ 2

5. Find the number of shapes in each row. Complete the addition sentence to find the total.

3 rows of ____

____ + ____ + ____ = ____

Operations and Algebraic Thinking

1. Which has the same value as 12 tens?

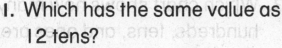

- ○ 2 tens
- ○ 1 hundred 1 ten
- ○ 1 hundred 2 tens
- ○ 2 hundreds

2. Which has the same value as 14 tens?

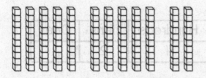

- ○ 4 tens
- ○ 40 tens
- ○ 1 hundred 4 tens
- ○ 1 hundred 14 tens

3. Which shows how many hundreds and tens?

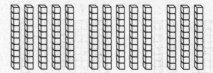

- ○ 1 hundred 3 tens
- ○ 1 hundred 4 tens
- ○ 1 hundred 8 tens
- ○ 2 hundreds 3 tens

4. Which shows how many hundreds and tens?

- ○ 1 hundred 1 ten
- ○ 1 hundred 5 tens
- ○ 5 hundreds 1 ten
- ○ 5 hundreds 5 tens

5. A number is made with 17 tens. Write the number in two different ways.

_____ hundred _____ tens

_____

Number and Operations in Base Ten

1. Kelly uses blocks to make the number 102. Which shows 102?

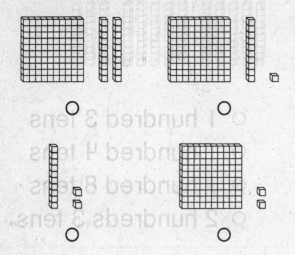

○   ○

○   ○

3. Which chart shows how many hundreds, tens, and ones are in 241?

○
Hundreds	Tens	Ones
4	2	1

○
Hundreds	Tens	Ones
2	4	1

○
Hundreds	Tens	Ones
1	4	2

○
Hundreds	Tens	Ones
2	1	4

2. What number is shown with these blocks?

○ 167

○ 252

○ 257

○ 262

4. Which chart shows how many hundreds, tens, and ones are in 423?

○
Hundreds	Tens	Ones
4	2	3

○
Hundreds	Tens	Ones
4	3	2

○
Hundreds	Tens	Ones
2	4	3

○
Hundreds	Tens	Ones
3	4	2

5. A model for a number has 2 hundreds blocks, 3 tens blocks, and no ones blocks. Complete the chart. Write the number.

Hundreds	Tens	Ones

_____

Number and Operations in Base Ten

1. Count the hundreds, tens, and ones. Which number does the picture show?

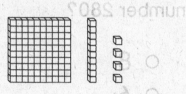

- ○ 441
- ○ 141
- ○ 414
- ○ 114

2. Which is a way to write the number shown with these blocks?

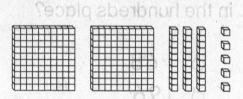

- ○ 200 + 20 + 5
- ○ 200 + 30 + 5
- ○ 300 + 20 + 5
- ○ 500 + 30 + 2

3. Liz has 248 beads. How many hundreds are in this number?

- ○ 2 hundreds
- ○ 4 hundreds
- ○ 6 hundreds
- ○ 8 hundreds

4. Ray sold 362 tickets to the show. Which is another way to write the number 362?

- ○ 6 hundreds 3 tens 2 ones
- ○ 3 hundreds 6 tens 3 ones
- ○ 3 hundreds 6 tens 2 ones
- ○ 2 hundreds 6 tens 3 ones

5. Write the number shown in the model in two different ways.

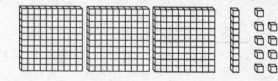

_____ + _____ + _____

_____

Number and Operations in Base Ten

1. A classroom has 537 books. What is the value of the digit 5 in 537?

   ○ 5
   ○ 50
   ○ 500
   ○ 537

2. There are 203 birds. What is the value of the digit 3 in the number 203?

   ○ 3
   ○ 30
   ○ 200
   ○ 300

3. Miss Brown drove 280 miles during summer vacation. What digit is in the tens place in the number 280?

   ○ 8
   ○ 6
   ○ 2
   ○ 0

4. Which number has the digit 6 in the hundreds place?

   ○ 68
   ○ 196
   ○ 362
   ○ 610

5. Write the value of the digit 9 in the number 890. Draw a quick picture to explain your answer.

   _____

1. The picture shows 20 tens.
   How many hundreds is this?

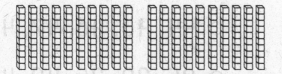

   ○ 2 hundreds
   ○ 20 hundreds
   ○ 200 hundreds
   ○ 210 hundreds

2. The picture shows 40 tens.
   How many hundreds is this?

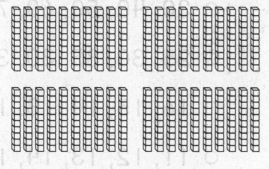

   ○ 410 hundreds
   ○ 400 hundreds
   ○ 40 hundreds
   ○ 4 hundreds

3. Which number has the same
   value as 50 tens?

   ○ 510
   ○ 500
   ○ 50
   ○ 5

4. Which number has the same
   value as 90 tens?

   ○ 910
   ○ 900
   ○ 90
   ○ 9

5. Write the number that has the same value as 30 tens.

   _____

1. Which group of numbers shows counting by fives?

  ○ 28, 27, 26, 25, 24

  ○ 35, 36, 37, 38, 39

  ○ 40, 50, 60, 70, 80

  ○ 55, 60, 65, 70, 75

3. Which group of numbers shows counting by ones?

  ○ 44, 45, 46, 47, 48

  ○ 25, 30, 35, 40, 45

  ○ 20, 30, 40, 50, 60

  ○ 10, 15, 20, 25, 30

2. Which group of numbers shows counting by tens?

  ○ 40, 41, 42, 44, 44

  ○ 50, 60, 70, 80, 90

  ○ 60, 65, 70, 75, 80

  ○ 70, 69, 68, 67, 66

4. Which group of numbers shows counting back by ones?

  ○ 30, 40, 50, 60, 70

  ○ 25, 30, 35, 30, 35

  ○ 16, 15, 14, 13, 12

  ○ 11, 12, 13, 14, 15

5. Write the missing numbers to show counting by tens.

  20, 30, _____, _____, _____, _____, _____

1. Which group of numbers shows counting by tens?

   ○ 610, 611, 612

   ○ 630, 640, 650

   ○ 635, 640, 645

   ○ 692, 691, 690

3. Which group of numbers shows counting by hundreds?

   ○ 500, 510, 520

   ○ 505, 510, 515

   ○ 400, 401, 402

   ○ 400, 500, 600

2. Which group of numbers shows counting by fives?

   ○ 340, 345, 350

   ○ 360, 361, 362

   ○ 430, 440, 450

   ○ 500, 600, 700

4. Which group of numbers shows counting back by ones?

   ○ 256, 257, 258

   ○ 225, 230, 235

   ○ 218, 217, 216

   ○ 190, 200, 210

5. Write the missing numbers to show counting by hundreds.

   300, 400, _____, _____, _____, _____, _____

1. What is the value of the underlined digit?

<u>2</u>7

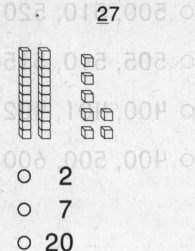

- ○ 2
- ○ 7
- ○ 20
- ○ 70

2. Lucas has 53 toy cars. What is the value of the digit 3 in the number 53?

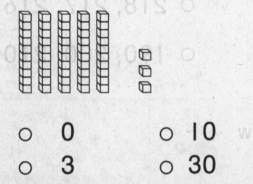

- ○ 0
- ○ 10
- ○ 3
- ○ 30

3. What is the value of the underlined digit?

4<u>8</u>

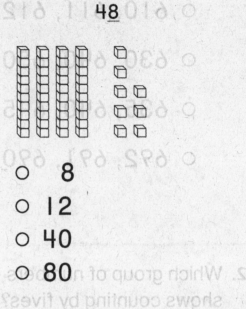

- ○ 8
- ○ 12
- ○ 40
- ○ 80

4. Ben has 62 crackers. What is the value of the 6 in this number?

- ○ 6
- ○ 8
- ○ 20
- ○ 60

5. Draw quick pictures for the missing blocks to show the number 36.

Number and Operations in Base Ten

1. Which shows another way to describe 27?

   ○ 20 + 7
   ○ 20 + 70
   ○ 2 + 7
   ○ 70 + 2

3. Which shows another way to describe 52?

   ○ 5 + 2
   ○ 20 + 5
   ○ 50 + 2
   ○ 500 + 2

2. Which shows another way to describe 65?

   ○ 5 tens 6 ones
   ○ 6 tens 0 ones
   ○ 6 tens 5 ones
   ○ 6 tens 6 ones

4. Which shows another way to describe 78?

   ○ 80 + 7
   ○ 70 + 8
   ○ 7 + 8
   ○ 80 + 70

5. Write the number.

   8 tens 4 ones
   80 + 4

   _____

Number and Operations in Base Ten

1. Which is another way to write thirty-eight?

   ○ 8 tens 3 ones
   ○ 38
   ○ 3 + 8
   ○ 83

3. Which is another way to write 5 tens 6 ones?

   ○ 60 + 5
   ○ fifty
   ○ 65
   ○ 50 + 6

2. Which is another way to write 10 + 9?

   ○ 9 tens 10 ones
   ○ 91
   ○ nineteen
   ○ ninety

4. Which is another way to write 72?

   ○ 7 tens 2 ones
   ○ seventy
   ○ 7 + 2
   ○ 7 + 20

5. Write the number 53 in two other ways.

   _____

   _____

1. The blocks show 29. How many tens and ones are there?

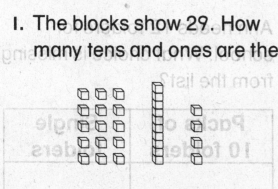

- ○ 2 tens 3 ones
- ○ 1 ten 19 ones
- ○ 1 ten 14 ones
- ○ 1 tens 9 ones

3. The blocks show 30. How many tens and ones are there?

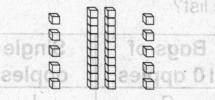

- ○ 1 ten 5 ones
- ○ 1 ten 10 ones
- ○ 2 tens 5 ones
- ○ 2 tens 10 ones

2. The blocks show 33. There are 2 tens and 13 ones. Which shows the number as tens plus ones?

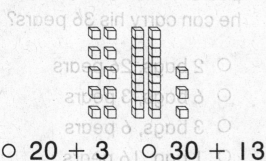

- ○ 20 + 3
- ○ 30 + 13
- ○ 20 + 13
- ○ 40 + 3

4. The blocks show 47. There are 3 tens and 17 ones. Which shows the number as tens plus ones?

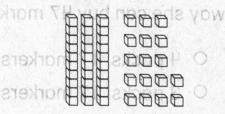

- ○ 20 + 17
- ○ 30 + 17
- ○ 30 + 7
- ○ 40 + 17

5. Describe the number 79 in two different ways.

_____ tens _____ ones

_____ + _____

Number and Operations in Base Ten

1. Jon wants to buy 21 apples. What choice is missing from the list?

Bags of 10 apples	Single apples
2	1
1	11

- ○ 0 bags, 21 apples
- ○ 0 bags, 11 apples
- ○ 1 bag, 21 apples
- ○ 2 bags, 2 apples

2. Ms. Brice can buy markers in packs of 10 or as single markers. Which of these is a way she can buy 47 markers?

- ○ 4 packs, 17 markers
- ○ 3 packs, 17 markers
- ○ 2 packs, 7 markers
- ○ 1 pack, 27 markers

3. Ann needs 12 folders for school. What choice is missing from the list?

Packs of 10 folders	Single folders
0	12

- ○ 2 packs, 0 folders
- ○ 2 packs, 1 folder
- ○ 1 pack, 12 folders
- ○ 1 pack, 2 folders

4. Jeff can carry his pears in bags of 10 pears or as single pears. Which of these is a way he can carry his 36 pears?

- ○ 2 bags, 26 pears
- ○ 6 bags, 3 pears
- ○ 3 bags, 6 pears
- ○ 1 bag, 16 pears

5. Stamps are sold in packs of 10 stamps or as single stamps. Leah wants to buy 26 stamps. What are all of the different ways she can buy the stamps?

Packs of 10 stamps	Single stamps

Number and Operations in Base Ten

1. There are five hundred twenty-three children at the school. Which shows this number?

   ○ 520
   ○ 523
   ○ 530
   ○ 532

2. Vin has three hundred forty pieces in his puzzle. Which shows this number?

   ○ 304
   ○ 314
   ○ 340
   ○ 341

3. Which is another way to write the number 275?

   ○ two hundred seventy-five
   ○ two hundred seventy
   ○ two hundred fifty-seven
   ○ two hundred five

4. Which is another way to write the number 618?

   ○ six hundred eight
   ○ six hundred eighteen
   ○ six hundred eighty-one
   ○ eight hundred sixteen

5. Write the number 454 using words.

   _____

1. Look at the picture.

Which shows how many hundreds, tens, and ones?

- ○ 2 hundreds 4 tens 3 ones
- ○ 3 hundreds 3 tens 4 ones
- ○ 3 hundreds 2 tens 4 ones
- ○ 2 hundreds 3 tens 4 ones

2. Claudia has four hundred sixty-five stickers in her collection. Which is another way to write the number?

- ○ 400 + 60 + 5
- ○ 400 + 600 + 5
- ○ 40 + 60 + 5
- ○ 4 + 6 + 5

3. Read the number and draw a quick picture. Then write the number in different ways.

three hundred sixty-five

_____ hundreds _____ tens _____ ones

_____ + _____ + _____

_____

Number and Operations in Base Ten

1. Which shows how many hundreds, tens, and ones are in 328?

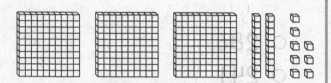

- ○
Hundreds	Tens	Ones
2	8	3

- ○
Hundreds	Tens	Ones
3	2	8

- ○
Hundreds	Tens	Ones
3	8	2

- ○
Hundreds	Tens	Ones
8	2	3

2. What number is shown with these blocks?

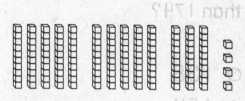

- ○ 413
- ○ 143
- ○ 134
- ○ 84

3. Write how many hundreds, tens, and ones are in the model.

211

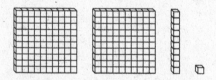

Hundreds	Tens	Ones

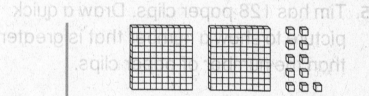

Hundreds	Tens	Ones

Number and Operations in Base Ten

1. There are 174 markers in a bin. Which number is greater than 174?

   ○ 138
   ○ 154
   ○ 147
   ○ 179

2. There are 213 books in the classroom. Which number is less than 213?

   ○ 231
   ○ 205
   ○ 276
   ○ 250

3. There are 332 puzzle pieces in a box. Which number is greater than 332?

   ○ 286
   ○ 241
   ○ 391
   ○ 323

4. There are 409 pennies in a jar. Which number is less than 409?

   ○ 390
   ○ 419
   ○ 437
   ○ 526

5. Tim has 128 paper clips. Draw a quick picture to show a number that is greater than the number of paper clips.

Hundreds	Tens	Ones

Hundreds	Tens	Ones

Number and Operations in Base Ten

1. Compare the numbers. Use >, <, or =.

Hundreds	Tens	Ones
2	4	1
2	1	4

241 ◯ 214

>   <   =
◯   ◯   ◯

2. Compare the numbers. Use >, <, or =.

Hundreds	Tens	Ones
4	1	4
4	4	0

414 ◯ 440

>   <   =
◯   ◯   ◯

3. Compare the numbers. Use >, <, or =.

638 ◯ 638

>   <   =
◯   ◯   ◯

4. Which of the following is greater than 357?

○ 140

○ 272

○ 346

○ 481

5. Mr. Lang has 437 stickers. Ms. Kim has 521 stickers. Who has more stickers? Write or draw to explain.

_____

1. What is the sum?

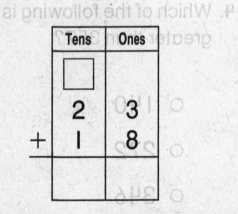

Tens	Ones
□ 7	5
+ 2	4

○ 83   ○ 99

○ 93   ○ 109

3. What is the sum?

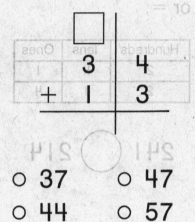

3 | 4
+ 1 | 3

○ 37   ○ 47

○ 44   ○ 57

2. What is the sum?

Tens	Ones
□ 2	3
+ 1	8

○ 41   ○ 31

○ 40   ○ 30

4. What is the sum?

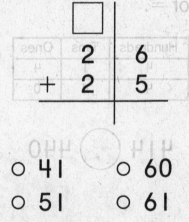

2 | 6
+ 2 | 5

○ 41   ○ 60

○ 51   ○ 61

5. Regroup if you need to.
Write the sum.

5 | 6
+ 2 | 8

© Houghton Mifflin Harcourt Publishing Company

Number and Operations in Base Ten

1. What is the sum?

$$\begin{array}{r} 5\ 8 \\ +\ \ 4\ 4 \\ \hline \end{array}$$

- ○ 92
- ○ 98
- ○ 102
- ○ 112

2. Elizabeth collected 72 markers. Tori collected 52 markers. How many markers did they collect in all?

$$\begin{array}{r} 7\ 2 \\ +\ \ 5\ 2 \\ \hline \end{array}$$

- ○ 114
- ○ 124
- ○ 130
- ○ 136

3. Tony found 31 shells on the beach. Andy found 27 shells. How many shells did they find in all?

$$\begin{array}{r} 3\ 1 \\ +\ \ 2\ 7 \\ \hline \end{array}$$

- ○ 46
- ○ 48
- ○ 54
- ○ 58

4. What is the sum?

$$\begin{array}{r} 8\ 8 \\ +\ \ 3\ 9 \\ \hline \end{array}$$

- ○ 117
- ○ 127
- ○ 131
- ○ 139

5. Curt sold 63 tickets to the concert. Art sold 49 tickets. How many tickets did they sell in all?

_____ tickets

1. What is the sum of 34 + 56?

   ○ 100
   ○ 90
   ○ 80
   ○ 74

3. What is the sum of 18 + 64?

   ○ 92
   ○ 84
   ○ 82
   ○ 72

2. What is the sum of 39 + 32?

   ○ 71
   ○ 68
   ○ 61
   ○ 51

4. What is the sum of 40 + 56?

   ○ 97
   ○ 96
   ○ 90
   ○ 86

5. Lynn scored 23 points in the basketball game. Shelly scored 28 points. How many points did they score in all?

_____ points

1. Break apart ones to subtract. What is the difference?

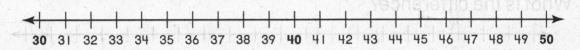

$$42 - 8 = \underline{\hspace{1.5cm}}$$

50	46	44	34
○	○	○	○

2. Break apart ones to subtract. What is the difference?

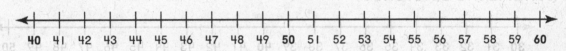

$$56 - 7 = \underline{\hspace{1.5cm}}$$

63	51	49	41
○	○	○	○

3. Harrison had 61 cars. He gave 6 cars to his brother. How many cars does Harrison have now?

- ○ 67
- ○ 57
- ○ 55
- ○ 54

4. Tracy had 33 stamps. She gave 5 stamps to her friend. How many stamps does Tracy have now?

- ○ 30
- ○ 28
- ○ 25
- ○ 18

5. Sam wants to subtract 9 from 47. How should he break apart the 9? Explain.

_____

_____

1. Break apart the number you are subtracting.
   What is the difference?

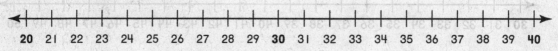

$$38 - 16 = \underline{\hspace{1cm}}$$

○ 32   ○ 22   ○ 12   ○ 2

2. Break apart the number you are subtracting.
   What is the difference?

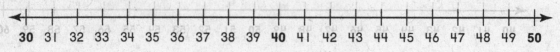

$$49 - 13 = \underline{\hspace{1cm}}$$

○ 62   ○ 46   ○ 42   ○ 36

3. Miles had 54 baseball cards.
   He gave 18 baseball cards to
   Greyson. How many baseball
   cards does Miles have now?

   ○ 44
   ○ 40
   ○ 38
   ○ 36

4. Last week Brooke made 28 bags
   for the festival. This week she
   made 14 bags. How many more
   bags did Brooke make last week
   than this week?

   ○ 52
   ○ 44
   ○ 14
   ○ 4

5. Break apart the number you are subtracting.
   Write the difference.

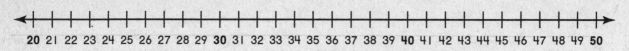

$$47 - 15 = \underline{\hspace{1cm}}$$

1. What is the difference?

Tens	Ones
□	□
4	7
− 1	6

○ 21   ○ 30

○ 29   ○ 31

2. What is the difference?

Tens	Ones
□	□
2	4
− 1	7

○ 17   ○ 7

○ 8   ○ 5

3. What is the difference?

Tens	Ones
□	□
6	1
− 2	8

○ 43   ○ 32

○ 33   ○ 23

4. Miguel read 36 pages today. He read 15 pages yesterday. How many more pages did he read today than yesterday?

○ 21   ○ 31

○ 23   ○ 51

5. Peter is subtracting 24 from 55. Explain why he does not need to regroup 1 ten as 10 ones.

_____

_____

1. Regroup if you need to.
What is the difference?

Tens	Ones
□	□
7	4
− 3	5

- ○ 49
- ○ 41
- ○ 39
- ○ 38

3. Regroup if you need to.
What is the difference?

Tens	Ones
□	□
8	6
− 2	8

- ○ 58
- ○ 59
- ○ 60
- ○ 68

2. Regroup if you need to.
What is the difference?

Tens	Ones
□	□
6	2
− 1	9

- ○ 81   ○ 41
- ○ 43   ○ 33

4. There were 43 cows in a field.
Then 16 cows went in a barn.
How many cows were still in
the field?

- ○ 59
- ○ 37
- ○ 29
- ○ 27

5. Write a subtraction problem that
you need to regroup to solve.
Explain why you need to regroup.

_____

_____

Number and Operations in Base Ten

1. What is the difference?

```
  6 0
− 2 1
```

- ○ 81
- ○ 49
- ○ 41
- ○ 39

3. What is the difference?

```
  6 7
− 2 6
```

- ○ 97
- ○ 83
- ○ 41
- ○ 31

2. What is the difference?

```
  2 8
− 1 5
```

- ○ 12
- ○ 13
- ○ 14
- ○ 15

4. What is the difference?

```
  5 0
− 2 6
```

- ○ 24
- ○ 25
- ○ 36
- ○ 76

5. When you subtract two 2-digit numbers, how do you know whether to regroup?

_____

_____

1. Which shows a different way to write the subtraction problem?

$$72 - 43$$

○ $\begin{array}{r} 72 \\ -\ 43 \\ \hline \end{array}$

○ $\begin{array}{r} 72 \\ -\ 34 \\ \hline \end{array}$

○ $\begin{array}{r} 27 \\ -\ 43 \\ \hline \end{array}$

○ $\begin{array}{r} 27 \\ -\ 34 \\ \hline \end{array}$

2. Which shows a different way to write the subtraction problem?

$$97 - 21$$

○ $\begin{array}{r} 97 \\ -\ 12 \\ \hline \end{array}$

○ $\begin{array}{r} 97 \\ -\ 21 \\ \hline \end{array}$

○ $\begin{array}{r} 79 \\ -\ 12 \\ \hline \end{array}$

○ $\begin{array}{r} 79 \\ -\ 21 \\ \hline \end{array}$

3. Which shows the answer to the subtraction problem?

$$59 - 12$$

○ 71

○ 57

○ 47

○ 41

4. Bill has 64 rocks. Tina has 39 rocks. How many more rocks does Bill have than Tina?

Write the subtraction problem two ways. Then find the difference.

_____

$\begin{array}{r} \\ -\ \\ \hline \end{array}$

_____ more rocks

1. Use the number line. Count up to find the difference. What is the difference?

$$84 - 75 = \underline{\qquad}$$

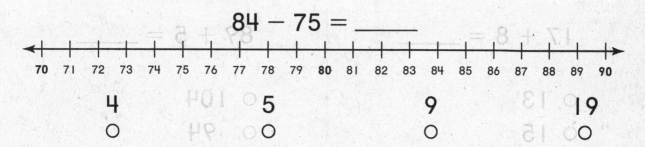

70 71 72 73 74 75 76 77 78 79 **80** 81 82 83 84 85 86 87 88 89 **90**

     4   5   9   19
     ○   ○   ○   ○

2. Use the number line. Count up to find the difference. What is the difference?

$$43 - 37 = \underline{\qquad}$$

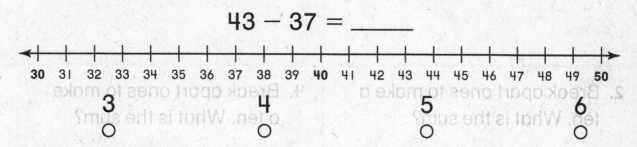

30 31 32 33 34 35 36 37 38 39 **40** 41 42 43 44 45 46 47 48 49 **50**

     3   4   5   6
     ○   ○   ○   ○

3. Use the number line. Count up to find the difference. What is the difference?

$$66 - 58 = \underline{\qquad}$$

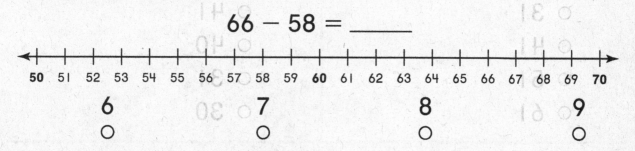

50 51 52 53 54 55 56 57 58 59 **60** 61 62 63 64 65 66 67 68 69 **70**

     6   7   8   9
     ○   ○   ○   ○

4. Amy needs to subtract 49 from 58. Explain how she can solve the problem by counting up.

_____

_____

_____

1. Break apart ones to make a ten. What is the sum?

$$17 + 8 = \underline{\hspace{1cm}}$$

- ○ 13
- ○ 15
- ○ 24
- ○ 25

3. Break apart ones to make a ten. What is the sum?

$$89 + 5 = \underline{\hspace{1cm}}$$

- ○ 104
- ○ 94
- ○ 84
- ○ 83

2. Break apart ones to make a ten. What is the sum?

$$57 + 4 = \underline{\hspace{1cm}}$$

- ○ 31
- ○ 41
- ○ 51
- ○ 61

4. Break apart ones to make a ten. What is the sum?

$$32 + 9 = \underline{\hspace{1cm}}$$

- ○ 41
- ○ 40
- ○ 31
- ○ 30

5. Break apart ones to make a ten. Write the sum.

$$27 + 7 = \underline{\hspace{1cm}}$$

Number and Operations in Base Ten

1. Which shows a way to find the sum?

$$41 + 29$$

○ $40 + 10 = 50$
○ $50 + 20 = 70$
○ $40 + 20 = 60$
○ $50 + 30 = 80$

3. Which shows a way to find the sum?

$$66 + 16$$

○ $60 + 16 = 76$
○ $70 + 16 = 86$
○ $60 + 12 = 72$
○ $70 + 12 = 82$

2. Which shows a way to find the sum?

$$38 + 18$$

○ $30 + 16 = 46$
○ $30 + 18 = 48$
○ $40 + 16 = 56$
○ $40 + 18 = 58$

4. Which shows a way to find the sum?

$$17 + 23$$

○ $10 + 20 = 30$
○ $10 + 23 = 33$
○ $17 + 20 = 37$
○ $10 + 30 = 40$

5. Make one addend the next tens number. Write the new addition sentence. Write the sum.

$$75 + 16$$

_____

_____

Number and Operations in Base Ten

1. Which shows how to break apart the addends to find the sum?

$$57 + 37$$

- ○ $50 + 30 + 7 + 7$
- ○ $50 + 20 + 7$
- ○ $20 + 14 + 7$
- ○ $30 + 7 + 7$

3. Which shows how to break apart the addends to find the sum?

$$45 + 18$$

- ○ $40 + 10 + 5$
- ○ $50 + 10 + 8 + 5$
- ○ $40 + 10 + 5 + 8$
- ○ $40 + 5 + 8$

2. Which shows how to break apart the addends to find the sum?

$$25 + 17$$

- ○ $20 + 10 + 7$
- ○ $20 + 10 + 5 + 7$
- ○ $30 + 10 + 5$
- ○ $20 + 7 + 5$

4. Which shows how to break apart the addends to find the sum?

$$49 + 23$$

- ○ $40 + 20 + 9 + 3$
- ○ $40 + 20 + 9$
- ○ $40 + 20 + 10$
- ○ $40 + 9 + 3$

5. Break apart the addends to find the sum.

$$67 \longrightarrow \underline{\qquad} + \underline{\qquad}$$

$$\underline{+\ 28} \longrightarrow \underline{\qquad} + \underline{\qquad}$$

$$\underline{\qquad} + \underline{\qquad} = \underline{\qquad}$$

Number and Operations in Base Ten

1. What is the sum?

Tens	Ones		Tens	Ones
☐				
1	6			
+ 1	8			

○ 23 ○ 33
○ 24 ○ 34

3. What is the sum?

Tens	Ones		Tens	Ones
☐				
3	4			
+ 2	6			

○ 54 ○ 60
○ 56 ○ 70

2. What is the sum?

Tens	Ones		Tens	Ones
☐				
5	9			
+ 2	7			

○ 86 ○ 76
○ 85 ○ 75

4. What is the sum?

Tens	Ones		Tens	Ones
☐				
4	4			
+ 2	8			

○ 52 ○ 68
○ 62 ○ 72

5. Draw quick pictures to help you solve. Write the sum.

Tens	Ones		Tens	Ones
☐				
2	3			
+ 6	8			

Number and Operations in Base Ten

1. What is the sum?

$$
\begin{array}{r}
58 \\
24 \\
+\ \ 3 \\
\hline
\end{array}
$$

○ 95　　○ 82
○ 85　　○ 27

3. What is the sum?

$$
\begin{array}{r}
54 \\
31 \\
+\ 17 \\
\hline
\end{array}
$$

○ 102　　○ 71
○ 85　　○ 48

2. What is the sum?

$$
\begin{array}{r}
62 \\
28 \\
+\ 11 \\
\hline
\end{array}
$$

○ 115　　○ 98
○ 101　　○ 91

4. What is the sum?

$$
\begin{array}{r}
48 \\
35 \\
+\ 24 \\
\hline
\end{array}
$$

○ 117　　○ 107
○ 111　　○ 99

5. Tom made 31 muffins for the bake sale. Sally made 58 muffins. Kyle made 9 muffins. How many muffins did they make in all?

_____ muffins

© Houghton Mifflin Harcourt Publishing Company

Number and Operations in Base Ten

1. What is the sum?

$$
\begin{array}{r}
34 \\
20 \\
11 \\
+\ 5 \\
\hline
\end{array}
$$

     ○ 78   ○ 69
     ○ 70   ○ 60

3. What is the sum?

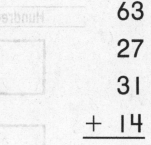

$$
\begin{array}{r}
63 \\
27 \\
31 \\
+\ 14 \\
\hline
\end{array}
$$

     ○ 135   ○ 125
     ○ 132   ○ 121

2. What is the sum?

$$
\begin{array}{r}
78 \\
43 \\
12 \\
+\ 4 \\
\hline
\end{array}
$$

     ○ 147   ○ 137
     ○ 143   ○ 127

4. What is the sum?

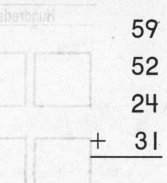

$$
\begin{array}{r}
59 \\
52 \\
24 \\
+\ 31 \\
\hline
\end{array}
$$

     ○ 174   ○ 162
     ○ 166   ○ 156

5. Keisha scored 51 points, 85 points,
    29 points, and 91 points on a
    computer game. How many points
    did Keisha score in all?

_____ points

1. Add 164 and 124. What is the sum?

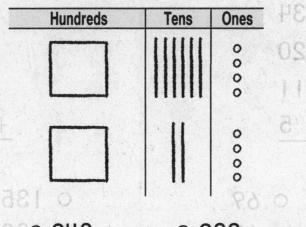

Hundreds	Tens	Ones

○ 140   ○ 248   ○ 288   ○ 298

2. Add 206 and 271. What is the sum?

Hundreds	Tens	Ones

○ 165   ○ 477   ○ 475   ○ 487

3. There are 331 ants on a picnic table.
Then 154 more ants join them.
How many ants are on the table now?
Draw quick pictures to help you solve
the problem. Then write the sum.

_____ ants

1. Which shows 681 broken apart
   into hundreds, tens, and ones?

   ○ 500 + 10 + 8
   ○ 500 + 80 + 1
   ○ 600 + 10 + 8
   ○ 600 + 80 + 1

2. Break apart the addends into hundreds,
   tens, and ones. What is the sum?

$$371$$
$$+ \ 148$$

   ○ 223   ○ 419   ○ 519   ○ 529

3. Break apart the addends into hundreds,
   tens, and ones. Add the hundreds, tens,
   and ones. Then find the sum.

   Theresa has 246 coins in her bank.
   Maggie has 137 coins in her bank.
   How many coins do they have altogther?

   246 ⟶ _____ + _____ + _____

   +137 ⟶ _____ + _____ + _____
   _____

   _____ + _____ + _____ = _____

© Houghton Mifflin Harcourt Publishing Company

1. What is the sum?

Hundreds	Tens	Ones
	☐	
3	7	5
+ 2	1	6

○ 691   ○ 581

○ 591   ○ 159

3. What is the sum?

Hundreds	Tens	Ones
	☐	
3	6	7
+ 1	2	8

○ 239   ○ 495

○ 485   ○ 595

2. What is the sum?

Hundreds	Tens	Ones
	☐	
1	4	9
+ 1	2	8

○ 267   ○ 278

○ 277   ○ 377

4. What is the sum?

Hundreds	Tens	Ones
	☐	
4	5	5
+ 2	3	5

○ 600   ○ 650

○ 610   ○ 690

5. Harry added two 3-digit numbers. He regrouped 18 ones as 1 ten 8 ones. Write two numbers that he could have added. Explain why he regrouped.

_____

_____

_____

© Houghton Mifflin Harcourt Publishing Company

Number and Operations in Base Ten

1. What is the sum?

Hundreds	Tens	Ones
☐	☐	
1	9	2
+ 3	5	6

- ○ 448
- ○ 458
- ○ 544
- ○ 548

3. What is the sum?

Hundreds	Tens	Ones
☐	☐	
1	8	3
+ 2	5	6

- ○ 439
- ○ 433
- ○ 349
- ○ 339

2. What is the sum?

Hundreds	Tens	Ones
☐	☐	
3	9	1
+ 2	9	6

- ○ 697
- ○ 687
- ○ 685
- ○ 587

4. What is the sum?

$$363$$
$$+254$$

- ○ 671
- ○ 651
- ○ 617
- ○ 607

5. Mike's Sports Shop has 398 baseballs and 121 basketballs. How many baseballs and basketballs does the shop have in all? Explain why you regrouped or did not regroup.

Hundreds	Tens	Ones
☐	☐	
+		

_____

_____

_____

1. What is the sum?

$$\begin{array}{r} 1\ 3\ 9 \\ +\ 3\ 7\ 9 \\ \hline \end{array}$$

○ 518   ○ 508
○ 500   ○ 418

3. What is the sum?

$$\begin{array}{r} 2\ 4\ 3 \\ +\ 4\ 5\ 7 \\ \hline \end{array}$$

○ 600   ○ 700
○ 690   ○ 790

2. What is the sum?

$$\begin{array}{r} 1\ 5\ 8 \\ +\ 1\ 6\ 2 \\ \hline \end{array}$$

○ 210   ○ 310
○ 220   ○ 320

4. What is the sum?

$$\begin{array}{r} 2\ 7\ 5 \\ +\ 1\ 6\ 8 \\ \hline \end{array}$$

○ 453   ○ 433
○ 443   ○ 343

5. There were 324 people at one movie. There were 396 people at another movie. How many people were at the two movies? Explain why you regrouped or did not regroup.

$$\begin{array}{r} 3\ 2\ 4 \\ +\ 3\ 9\ 6 \\ \hline \end{array}$$

_____

_____

_____ people

1. There were 487 cars in a parking lot.
   Then 156 cars left. How many cars are
   in the parking lot now?

   ○ 231   ○ 321   ○ 331   ○ 336

2. Helen counted 381 leaves on her porch.
   There were 129 red leaves. How many
   leaves were not red?

   ○ 262   ○ 252   ○ 250   ○ 249

3. There were 614 boxes at a post office.
   Then people took 280 boxes home. How
   many boxes are still at the post office?

   ○ 434   ○ 420   ○ 344   ○ 334

4. Michael collected 525 bottle caps. His sister
   collected 413 bottle caps. How many more
   bottle caps did Michael collect than his sister?
   Draw a quick picture to help you solve the
   problem. Then write your answer.

   _____ more bottle caps

1. What is the difference?

Hundreds	Tens	Ones
	☐	☐
7	9	5
− 5	3	7

- ○ 257
- ○ 258
- ○ 267
- ○ 268

2. What is the difference?

Hundreds	Tens	Ones
	☐	☐
5	5	7
− 4	1	9

- ○ 138
- ○ 142
- ○ 148
- ○ 156

3. Mr. Hansen needs to subtract 145 from 783.
Should he regroup? Explain why or why not.
Then find the difference.

_____

_____

_____

_____

_____

_____

Number and Operations in Base Ten

1. What is the difference?

$$\begin{array}{r} 8\ 4\ 7 \\ -\ 3\ 9\ 2 \\ \hline \end{array}$$

- ○ 559
- ○ 539
- ○ 555
- ○ 455

2. What is the difference?

$$\begin{array}{r} 4\ 1\ 3 \\ -\ 1\ 5\ 2 \\ \hline \end{array}$$

- ○ 261
- ○ 345
- ○ 341
- ○ 565

3. What is the difference?

$$\begin{array}{r} 5\ 4\ 8 \\ -\ 2\ 7\ 6 \\ \hline \end{array}$$

- ○ 262
- ○ 372
- ○ 272
- ○ 374

4. What is the difference?

$$\begin{array}{r} 9\ 2\ 4 \\ -\ 4\ 6\ 0 \\ \hline \end{array}$$

- ○ 584
- ○ 464
- ○ 544
- ○ 440

5. Sally wants to subtract 461 from 629. Should she regroup? Explain. Then find the difference.

_____

_____

_____

_____

_____

1. What is the difference?

$$
\begin{array}{r}
7\ 2\ 5 \\
-\ 2\ 8\ 4 \\
\hline
\end{array}
$$

- ○ 441
- ○ 541
- ○ 449
- ○ 545

3. What is the difference?

$$
\begin{array}{r}
8\ 5\ 2 \\
-\ 6\ 7\ 6 \\
\hline
\end{array}
$$

- ○ 276
- ○ 176
- ○ 186
- ○ 174

2. What is the difference?

$$
\begin{array}{r}
5\ 6\ 1 \\
-\ 1\ 9\ 3 \\
\hline
\end{array}
$$

- ○ 358
- ○ 458
- ○ 368
- ○ 468

4. What is the difference?

$$
\begin{array}{r}
6\ 3\ 7 \\
-\ 4\ 5\ 8 \\
\hline
\end{array}
$$

- ○ 175
- ○ 189
- ○ 179
- ○ 271

5. Subtract 189 from 445. Explain how to find the difference. Include regrouping if needed.

$$
\begin{array}{r}
4\ 4\ 5 \\
-\ 1\ 8\ 9 \\
\hline
\end{array}
$$

_____

_____

_____

_____

1. What is the difference?

```
    3 0 6
  − 1 2 7
```

○ 289   ○ 179

○ 189   ○ 171

3. What is the difference?

```
    4 4 8
  − 2 6 3
```

○ 185   ○ 285

○ 195   ○ 291

2. What is the difference?

```
    9 0 2
  − 5 3 8
```

○ 464   ○ 374

○ 382   ○ 364

4. What is the difference?

```
    7 0 4
  − 3 5 5
```

○ 459   ○ 349

○ 449   ○ 341

5. Write the difference. Did you regroup? Explain.

```
    6 0 7
  − 2 1 9
```

_____

_____

_____

_____

1. Which number is 10 more than 837?

   ○ 827
   ○ 847
   ○ 937
   ○ 947

3. Which number is 100 more than 326?

   ○ 226
   ○ 336
   ○ 426
   ○ 436

2. Which number is 10 less than 619?

   ○ 629
   ○ 610
   ○ 609
   ○ 519

4. Which number is 100 less than 541?

   ○ 641
   ○ 531
   ○ 451
   ○ 441

5. Write numbers to make the sentences true.

   _____ is _____ less than 681.

   _____ is _____ less than 681.

1. Look at the pattern. What number comes next?

   321, 331, 341, 351

   ○ 311
   ○ 352
   ○ 361
   ○ 362

3. Look at the pattern. What two numbers come next in the pattern?

   467, 477, 487, 497

   ○ 507, 517
   ○ 517, 527
   ○ 587, 597
   ○ 597, 697

2. Rico wrote this number pattern. What two numbers come next in Rico's pattern?

   183, 283, 383, 483

   ○ 493, 503
   ○ 683, 783
   ○ 484, 485
   ○ 583, 683

4. Beth wrote a number pattern starting with 325. She counted on by hundreds. Which of the following numbers comes next in her number pattern?

   ○ 225
   ○ 335
   ○ 415
   ○ 425

5. Write the next two numbers in this pattern.

   231, 241, 251, 261, _____, _____

Number and Operations in Base Ten

1. Add 65 and 9. How many tens are in the sum?

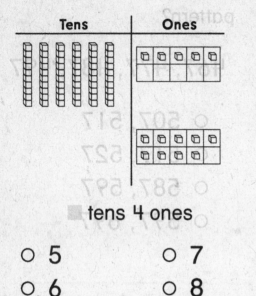

■ tens 4 ones

○ 5   ○ 7
○ 6   ○ 8

2. Add 45 and 16. How many ones are in the sum?

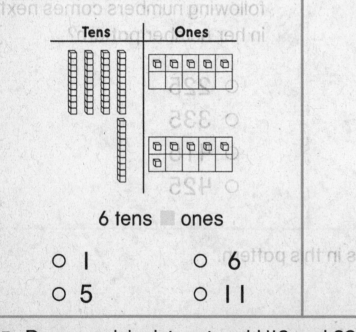

6 tens ■ ones

○ 1   ○ 6
○ 5   ○ 11

3. Add 29 and 17. What is the sum?

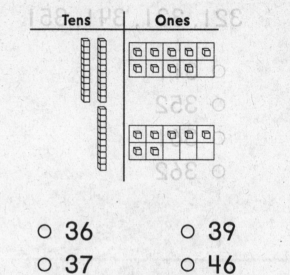

○ 36   ○ 39
○ 37   ○ 46

4. Add 28 and 39. What is the sum?

Tens	Ones

○ 57   ○ 67
○ 66   ○ 69

5. Draw a quick picture to add 42 and 29. Write the sum.

_____

1. Subtract 16 from 52. What is the difference?

Tens	Ones

○ 69   ○ 36

○ 44   ○ 34

2. Subtract 14 from 43. Which shows the tens and ones in the difference?

Tens	Ones

○ 2 tens 9 ones

○ 3 tens 1 one

○ 5 tens 7 ones

○ 8 tens 7 ones

3. Subtract 27 from 43. What is the difference?

Tens	Ones

○ 70   ○ 16

○ 24   ○ 14

4. Draw to show the regrouping. Write the tens and ones that are in the difference. Write the number.

Subtract 28 from 54.

Tens	Ones

_____ tens _____ ones

_____

1. Use color tiles. About how many inches long is the string?

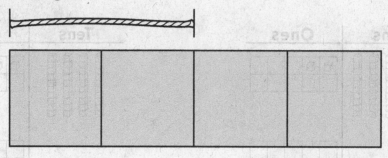

- ○ about 1 inch
- ○ about 2 inches
- ○ about 3 inches
- ○ about 4 inches

2. Use color tiles. About how many inches long is the ribbon?

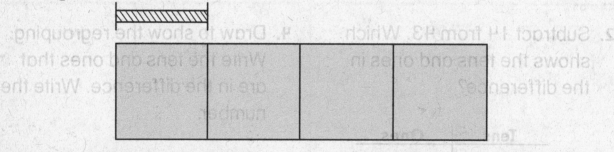

- ○ about 5 inches
- ○ about 4 inches
- ○ about 2 inches
- ○ about 1 inch

3. Use color tiles. Write the length of the pencil in inches.

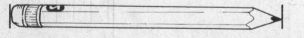

about _____ inches

1. Each square tile is about 1 inch long. How long is the ribbon?

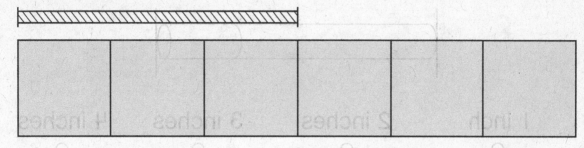

- ○ about 1 inch
- ○ about 2 inches
- ○ about 3 inches
- ○ about 4 inches

2. Each square tile is about 1 inch long. How long is the string?

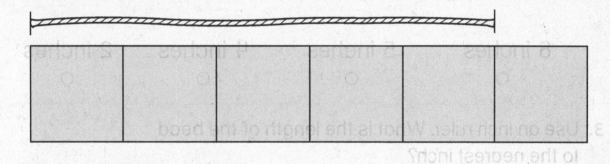

- ○ about 3 inches
- ○ about 4 inches
- ○ about 5 inches
- ○ about 6 inches

3. Each square tile is about 1 inch long. Write the length of the marker in inches.

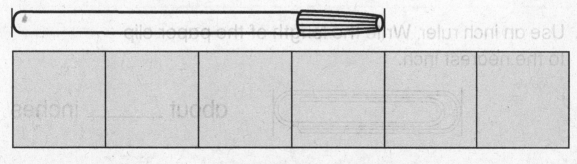

about _____ inches

Measurement and Data

1. Use an inch ruler. What is the length of the marker to the nearest inch?

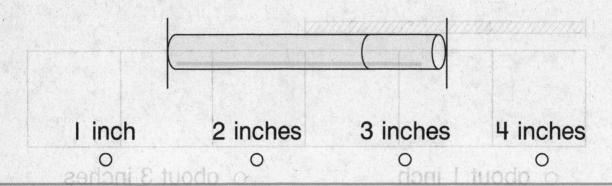

1 inch	2 inches	3 inches	4 inches
○	○	○	○

2. Use an inch ruler. What is the length of the string to the nearest inch?

8 inches	5 inches	4 inches	2 inches
○	○	○	○

3. Use an inch ruler. What is the length of the bead to the nearest inch?

1 inch	2 inches	3 inches	4 inches
○	○	○	○

4. Use an inch ruler. Write the length of the paper clip to the nearest inch.

about _____ inches

1. Sam wants to measure the distance around a soup can. Which is the best tool for Sam to use?

o yardstick
o measuring tape
o large paper clip
o inch ruler

3. Stacey wants to measure some paintbrushes to find one that is 6 inches long. Which is the best tool for her to use?

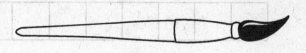

o inch ruler
o paper clip
o yardstick
o unit cubes

2. Taylor wants to measure the length of the school hallway. Which is the best tool for him to use?

o inch ruler
o centimeter ruler
o yardstick
o unit cubes

4. Angelina wants to measure the distance around her basketball. Which is the best tool for her to use?

o inch ruler
o measuring tape
o unit cubes
o yardstick

5. Draw a picture of something you would use a centimeter ruler to measure.

Measurement and Data

1. Eric used unit cubes to measure the length of a ribbon. Each unit cube is about 1 centimeter long. About how long is the ribbon?

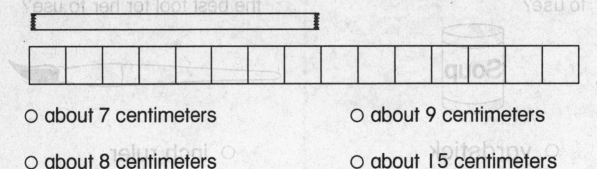

○ about 7 centimeters   ○ about 9 centimeters

○ about 8 centimeters   ○ about 15 centimeters

2. Ken used unit cubes to measure the length of a stick. Each unit cube is about 1 centimeter long. About how long is the stick?

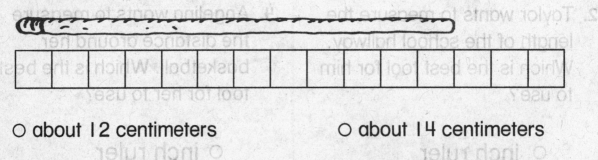

○ about 12 centimeters   ○ about 14 centimeters

○ about 13 centimeters   ○ about 15 centimeters

3. Each unit cube is about 1 centimeter long. Draw a line below the unit cubes. Tell how long the line you drew is.

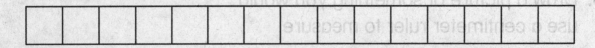

My line is about _____ centimeters long.

Measurement and Data

1. Use a centimeter ruler. What is the length of the pen cap to the nearest centimeter?

8 centimeters   7 centimeters   6 centimeters   5 centimeters
   ○   ○   ○   ○

2. Use a centimeter ruler. What is the length of the fish to the nearest centimeter?

8 centimeters   10 centimeters   12 centimeters   16 centimeters
   ○   ○   ○   ○

3. Use a centimeter ruler. What is the length of the ribbon to the nearest centimeter?

5 centimeters   7 centimeters   8 centimeters   9 centimeters
   ○   ○   ○   ○

4. Use a centimeter ruler. What is the length of the leaf to the nearest centimeter? Explain your answer.

_____

_____

1. Which of the following makes the sentence correct?

   I foot is _____ I inch.

   ○ the same as
   ○ shorter than
   ○ longer than

2. Mia measures the length of a book to the nearest inch. It is about 12 inches long. How long is the book?

   ○ I foot
   ○ 2 feet
   ○ 6 feet
   ○ 12 feet

3. Lee has a string that is 3 inches long. Pat has a string that is 3 feet long. Which of the following is correct?

   ○ Lee's string is longer.
   ○ Pat's string is longer.
   ○ Both strings are the same length.

4. Pedro measures the length of a stick to the nearest foot. It is about I foot long. About how many inches long is the stick?

   _____ inches

Measurement and Data

1. Which makes the sentence correct?

   I centimeter is _____ I meter.

   ○ the same as
   ○ shorter than
   ○ longer than

2. Tina measures the length of a table to the nearest meter. It is about I meter long. About how many centimeters long is the table?

   ○　　I centimeter
   ○　　5 centimeters
   ○　10 centimeters
   ○　100 centimeters

3. Which is the best choice for the length of a real bookshelf?

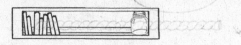

   ○ I centimeter　　○ 10 centimeters　　○ I meter　　○ 10 meters

4. Would you measure the length of a real car in meters or centimeters? Explain why.

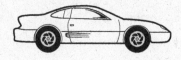

   _____

   _____

   _____

1. Lily has some beads that are 1 inch long each.
She wants to put them on a string.

Which is the best estimate for the length of the string?

5 inches	3 inches	2 inches	1 inch
○	○	○	○

2. Leo has some beads that are 1 inch long each.
He wants to put them on a string.

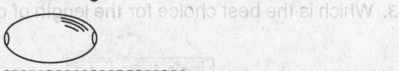

Which is the best estimate for the length of the string?

1 inch	2 inches	3 inches	4 inches
○	○	○	○

3. Ann has some beads that are 1 inch long each.
She wants to put them on a string.

Circle the best estimate for the length of the string.

10 inches	5 inches	3 inches	1 inch

1. Which is the best estimate of the length of a real kitchen table?

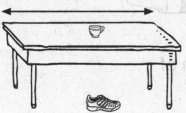

- ○ 1 foot
- ○ 4 feet
- ○ 12 feet
- ○ 20 feet

2. Which is the best estimate of the length of a real folder?

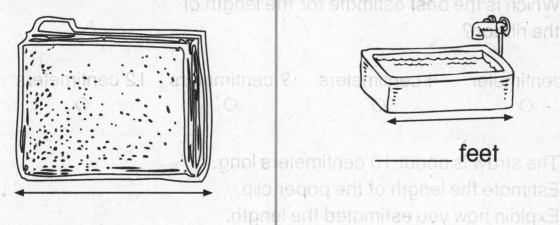

- ○ 10 feet
- ○ 5 feet
- ○ 3 feet
- ○ 1 foot

3. Which is the best estimate of the length of a real baseball bat?

- ○ 10 feet
- ○ 7 feet
- ○ 3 feet
- ○ 1 foot

4. Write the best estimate of the length of a real bathtub.

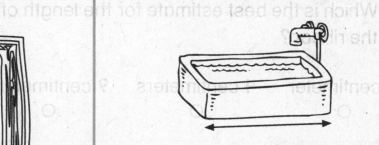

_____ feet

1. The length of the string is about 3 centimeters.

Which is the best estimate for the length of
the crayon?

1 centimeter	2 centimeters	4 centimeters	7 centimeters
○	○	○	○

2. The pencil is about 8 centimeters long.

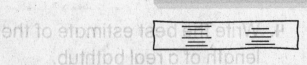

Which is the best estimate for the length of
the ribbon?

1 centimeter	4 centimeters	9 centimeters	12 centimeters
○	○	○	○

3. The straw is about 10 centimeters long.
   Estimate the length of the paper clip.
   Explain how you estimated the length.

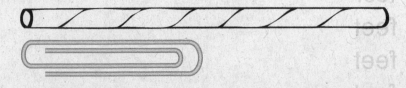

_____

_____

© Houghton Mifflin Harcourt Publishing Company

Measurement and Data

I. Which is the best estimate for the width of a real stove?

- ○ about 4 meters
- ○ about 2 meters
- ○ about 3 meters
- ○ about I meter

2. Which is the best estimate for the length of a real bus?

- ○ about 3 meters
- ○ about 6 meters
- ○ about 4 meters
- ○ about 12 meters

3. Think about a room in your home. How would you estimate its length in meters?

_____

_____

_____

_____

1. Measure the length of each object. How much longer is the celery than the carrot?

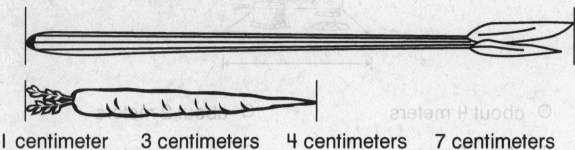

1 centimeter	3 centimeters	4 centimeters	7 centimeters
○	○	○	○

2. Which number sentence can be used to find how much longer the ribbon is than the paper clip?

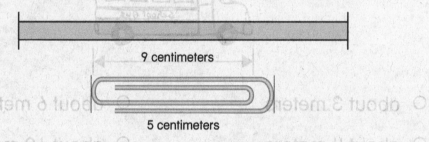

9 centimeters

5 centimeters

○ $9 + 5 = 14$ ○ $9 - 5 = 4$

○ $9 + 4 = 13$ ○ $5 - 4 = 1$

3. Write a problem about measures. Then subtract.

_____ is _____ centimeters long.

_____ is _____ centimeters long.

What is the difference in the lengths?

_____

_____

1. Mr. Owen has a board that is 17 inches long. Then he cuts 8 inches off the board. How long is the board now?

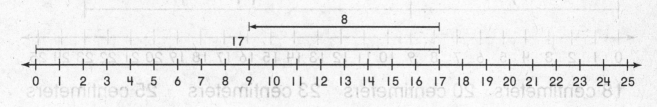

9 inches   11 inches   17 inches   20 inches
○   ○   ○   ○

2. Juan has a cube train that is 13 inches long. He removes 5 inches of the cube train. How long is the cube train now?

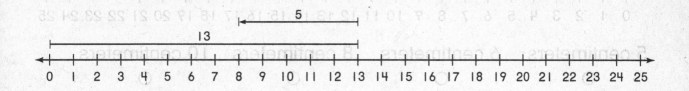

18 inches   13 inches   8 inches   7 inches
○   ○   ○   ○

3. Meg has a ribbon that is 9 inches long and another ribbon that is 12 inches long. How many inches of ribbon does Meg have in all?

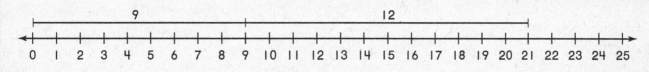

_____ inches

1. Karen has a toy car that is 9 centimeters long. She has a toy truck that is 14 centimeters long. She puts them end-to-end. How long are the car and truck together?

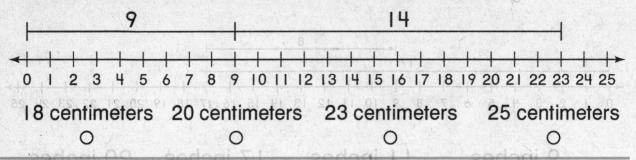

○ 18 centimeters   ○ 20 centimeters   ○ 23 centimeters   ○ 25 centimeters

2. Matt had a fruit roll that was 13 centimeters long. Then he ate 7 centimeters of the fruit roll. How long is the fruit roll now?

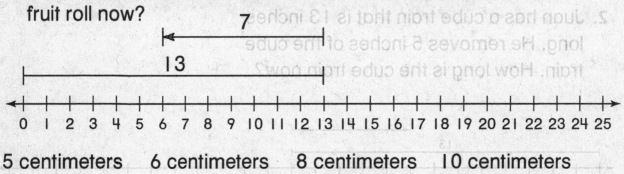

○ 5 centimeters   ○ 6 centimeters   ○ 8 centimeters   ○ 10 centimeters

3. Amy drew this diagram to show a problem about lengths in centimeters.

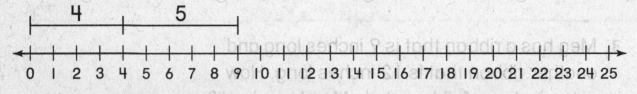

Write a problem that Amy might be trying to solve.
Solve the problem.

_____

_____

_____

_____ centimeters

Measurement and Data

1. Petra's soccer practice starts at 5:00.
   Which clock shows this time?

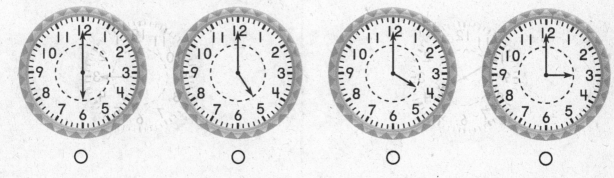

    ○   ○   ○   ○

2. Lee leaves school at 2:30. Which clock
   shows this time?

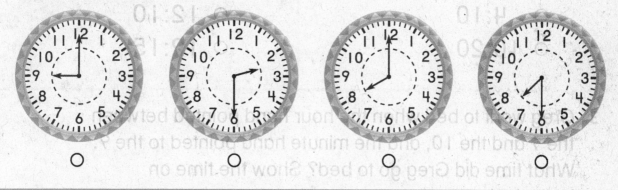

    ○   ○   ○   ○

3. Yolanda leaves for school when the hour hand points
   halfway between the 7 and 8, and the minute hand
   points to the 6. What time does Yolanda leave for
   school? Show the time on both clocks.

Measurement and Data

1. What is the time on the clock?

- ○ 3:40
- ○ 3:50
- ○ 4:10
- ○ 10:20

2. What is the time on the clock?

- ○ 3:15
- ○ 3:00
- ○ 12:10
- ○ 12:15

3. Greg went to bed when the hour hand pointed between the 9 and the 10, and the minute hand pointed to the 9. What time did Greg go to bed? Show the time on both clocks.

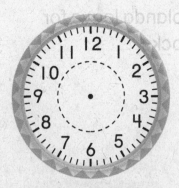

Measurement and Data

1. Which clock shows half past 7?

 ○   ○   ○   ○

2. Which clock shows ten minutes after 2?

 ○   ○   ○   ○

3. Terry's mother looked at a clock. "It's half past 8," she said. "We have to go!" What time did the clock show? Show the time on both clocks. Then write the time another way.

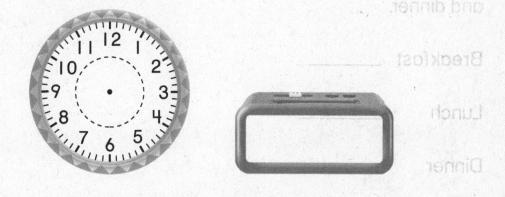

1. Rhonda saw a movie last night. The clock shows when the movie ended.

What time did the movie end?

- ○ 9:35 P.M.
- ○ 9:45 P.M.
- ○ 9:25 A.M.
- ○ 9:35 A.M.

2. Keisha has a math test today. The clock shows when the test starts.

What time does the test start?

- ○ 11:10 P.M.
- ○ 11:20 P.M.
- ○ 11:05 A.M.
- ○ 11:10 A.M.

3. Write the times you usually eat breakfast, lunch, and dinner.

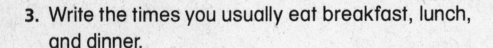

Breakfast _____

Lunch _____

Dinner _____

1. What is the total value of these coins?

8¢	24¢	28¢	40¢
○	○	○	○

2. What is the total value of these coins?

50¢	40¢	35¢	25¢
○	○	○	○

3. Sharon has these coins. What is the total value of Sharon's coins?

26¢	41¢	46¢	51¢
○	○	○	○

4. Draw coins to show 40¢.

Measurement and Data

1. Fred has these coins in his pocket.

   How much money does Fred have in his pocket?

   49¢   54¢   59¢   95¢
   ○   ○   ○   ○

2. What is the total value of these coins?

   62¢   71¢   72¢   77¢
   ○   ○   ○   ○

3. What is the total value of these coins?

   73¢   80¢   83¢   88¢
   ○   ○   ○   ○

4. Draw coins to show 56¢.
   Use as few coins as possible.

1. What is the total value of these coins?
You can draw and label the coins from
greatest to **least** value.

　　74¢　　　　　79¢　　　　　81¢　　　　　84¢
　　　○　　　　　　○　　　　　　○　　　　　　○

2. Mike has these coins in his wallet.

What is the total value of the coins
in Mike's wallet?

　　21¢　　　　　29¢　　　　　42¢　　　　　47¢
　　　○　　　　　　○　　　　　　○　　　　　　○

3. Draw coins to show 71¢. Show your coins
in order from greatest to least value.

1. Which coin will make the amounts equal?

     ? _____

 ○    ○    ○    ○

2. Which coin will make the amounts equal?

      ? _____

 ○    ○   ○    ○

3. Lucy needs 29¢ to buy a pencil. Draw coins to show two different ways Lucy can make 29¢.

Measurement and Data

1. Which group of coins has a total value of $1.00?

2. Jessie has these coins.

   Which coin does she need to make $1.00?

3. Lawrence paid $1.00 for a juice drink.
   He paid with only dimes and nickels.
   Draw the coins he could have used.

1. What is the total value of this money?

$1.07	$1.15	$1.22	$1.27
○	○	○	○

2. What is the total value of these coins?

$1.46	$1.36	$1.31	$1.26
○	○	○	○

3. What is the total value of this money?

$1.45	$1.50	$1.55	$1.60
○	○	○	○

4. Heather bought a toy car for $1.63.
Draw a bill and coins to show the
money she could have used.

1. Molly has 3 quarters, 3 dimes, and
   4 nickels in her coin bank. How much
   money does she have?

   $1.15 $1.20 $1.25 $1.40
   ○   ○   ○   ○

2. Tim spent two $1 bills, 2 quarters,
   1 nickel, and 3 pennies at a fair.
   How much money did he spend?

   $2.30 $2.33 $2.53 $2.58
   ○   ○   ○   ○

3. Chris gave his sister three $1 bills,
   4 quarters, 1 dime, and 2 pennies.
   How much money did he give his sister?

   $3.97 $4.12 $4.17 $4.25
   ○   ○   ○   ○

4. Bill wants to buy a model car that costs
   $3.65. Draw bills and coins to show the
   money he could use to buy the car.

**Use the line plot
for Questions 1–4.**

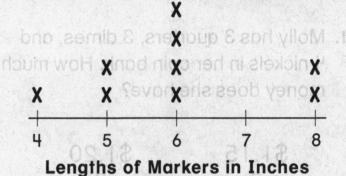

Lengths of Markers in Inches

1. How many markers are
   4 inches long?
   - o 1
   - o 4
   - o 6
   - o 8

3. How many markers are
   7 inches long?
   - o 7
   - o 2
   - o 1
   - o 0

2. How many markers does the
   line plot show?
   - o 10
   - o 9
   - o 8
   - o 4

4. How many inches long is the
   longest marker?
   - o 5
   - o 6
   - o 8
   - o 9

5. Dana found 3 markers that measure 7 inches.
   How would you change the line plot to show
   the markers Dana found?

   _____

   _____

Amber asked her classmates about their favorite flavor of yogurt. Use the tally chart for 1–4.

Favorite Yogurt Flavor	
Yogurt	**Tally**
peach	|||
berry	~~||||~~
lime	||
vanilla	~~||||~~ ||

1. How many classmates chose berry?
   - ○ 2
   - ○ 3
   - ○ 5
   - ○ 6

2. Which flavor did the **fewest** classmates choose?
   - ○ berry
   - ○ lime
   - ○ vanilla
   - ○ peach

3. Which statement is true?
   - ○ More classmates chose lime than peach.
   - ○ More classmates chose vanilla than berry.
   - ○ Fewer classmates chose vanilla than lime.
   - ○ Fewer classmates chose vanilla than peach.

4. What is another question you can ask based on the tally chart? Write your question and then answer it.

_____

_____

Measurement and Data

Use the picture graph for 1–5.

Favorite Recess Game									
tag	☺	☺							
catch	☺	☺	☺	☺	☺	☺	☺	☺	☺
kickball	☺	☺	☺	☺	☺	☺			
jacks	☺	☺	☺	☺					

Key: Each ☺ stands for 1 child.

1. Which game did the **most** children choose?

   ○ tag
   ○ kickball
   ○ catch
   ○ jacks

2. How many children in all chose tag or jacks?

   ○ 15
   ○ 9
   ○ 6
   ○ 3

3. How many children chose kickball?

   ○ 3
   ○ 6
   ○ 9
   ○ 15

4. How many more children chose catch than kickball?

   ○ 3
   ○ 4
   ○ 5
   ○ 7

5. How many children chose a recess game? Explain how you know.

_____

_____

© Houghton Mifflin Harcourt Publishing Company

Measurement and Data

Use the tally chart and picture graph for 1–5.

Favorite Vegetable	
Fruit	Tally
carrot	卌
lettuce	|||
tomato	卌	
pepper	||

Favorite Vegetable					
carrot	☺	☺	☺	☺	☺
lettuce					
tomato					
pepper					

Key: Each ☺ stands for 1 child.

1. How many ☺ should be in the picture graph next to pepper?
   - ○ 2
   - ○ 3
   - ○ 5
   - ○ 6

3. How many ☺ should be in the picture graph next to tomato?
   - ○ 7
   - ○ 6
   - ○ 4
   - ○ 3

2. How many ☺ should be in the picture graph next to lettuce?
   - ○ 1
   - ○ 2
   - ○ 3
   - ○ 6

4. How many fewer children chose pepper than tomato?
   - ○ 1
   - ○ 2
   - ○ 3
   - ○ 4

5. How is the tally chart like the picture graph?

_____

_____

Use the bar graph
for 1–5.

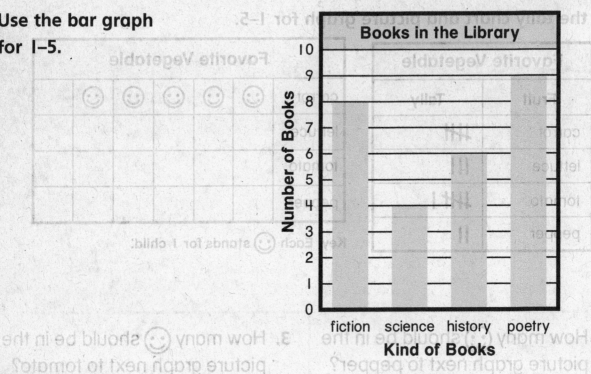

Books in the Library

Number of Books

10
9
8
7
6
5
4
3
2
1
0

fiction   science   history   poetry

Kind of Books

---

1. How many more history books than science books are in the library?
   - ○ 10
   - ○ 6
   - ○ 4
   - ○ 2

2. How many fiction books are in the library?
   - ○ 4
   - ○ 5
   - ○ 8
   - ○ 9

3. How many books are in the library in all?
   - ○ 27
   - ○ 26
   - ○ 23
   - ○ 17

4. Which kind of book does the library have the fewest of?
   - ○ fiction
   - ○ science
   - ○ history
   - ○ poetry

5. Can you answer question 4 without reading any numbers on the graph? Explain.

_____

_____

Measurement and Data

Use the information for 1–2.

Jorge is making a bar graph about summer sports.

- 5 children played tennis.

- 4 children played baseball.

- 2 children played basketball.

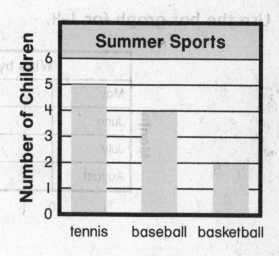

1. Which could be the missing label in the bar graph?

   ○ Number of Children
   ○ Type of Sport
   ○ Tennis
   ○ Soccer

2. How many more children played tennis than played basketball?

   ○ 1   ○ 3
   ○ 2   ○ 4

3. Tina is making a bar graph to show the number of notebooks her friends have.

- Lara has 4 notebooks.

- Marta has 3 notebooks.

- John has 1 notebook.

Write labels and draw bars to complete the graph.

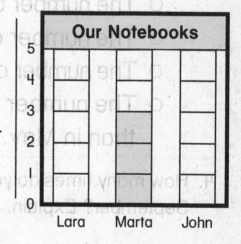

Use the bar graph for 1–4.

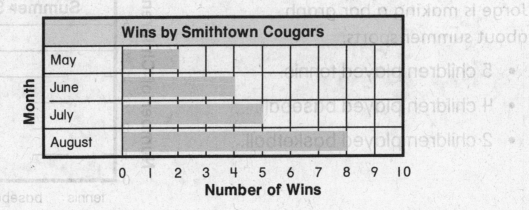

1. How many times did the Cougars win in May?

   ○ 8
   ○ 5
   ○ 4
   ○ 2

2. How many more wins did the Cougars have in August than in July?

   ○ 6   ○ 3
   ○ 4   ○ 2

3. Which of the following describes how the number of wins changed from May to August?

   ○ The number of wins increased each month.
   ○ The number of wins decreased each month.
   ○ The number of wins stayed about the same.
   ○ The number of wins in August was 8 more than in May.

4. How many times do you think the Cougars will win in September? Explain.

   _____

   _____

   _____

1. Which of these shapes is a cube?

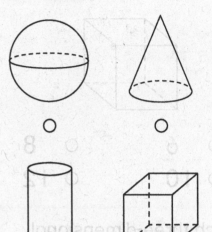

○   ○

○   ○

2. Which of these shapes is a sphere?

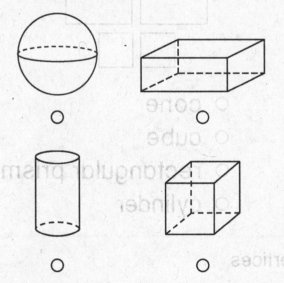

○   ○

○   ○

3. Which of these shapes is a cone?

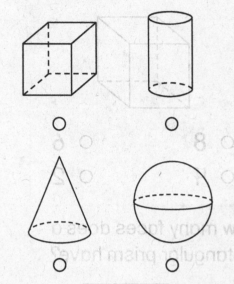

○   ○

○   ○

4. Which shape does *not* roll?

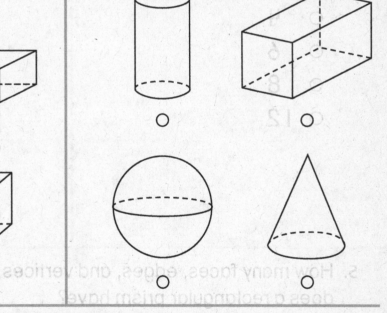

○   ○

○   ○

5. Draw an X on the shapes that roll.

   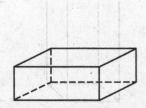

Geometry

1. How many vertices does a cube have?

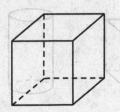

- ○ 8
- ○ 6
- ○ 4
- ○ 2

3. How many edges does a cube have?

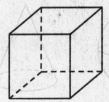

- ○ 6
- ○ 8
- ○ 10
- ○ 12

2. How many faces does a rectangular prism have?

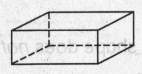

- ○ 4
- ○ 6
- ○ 8
- ○ 12

4. Which three-dimensional shape could you make with these faces?

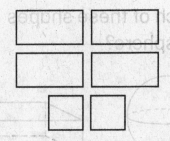

- ○ cone
- ○ cube
- ○ rectangular prism
- ○ cylinder

5. How many faces, edges, and vertices does a rectangular prism have?

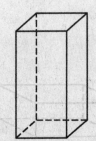

_____ faces

_____ edges

_____ vertices

Geometry

1. How many vertices does a triangle have?

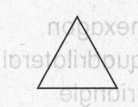

  ○ 1   ○ 2
  ○ 3   ○ 4

2. Which names a shape with 6 sides and 6 vertices?

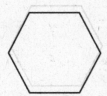

  ○ hexagon
  ○ pentagon
  ○ quadrilateral
  ○ triangle

3. How many sides does a quadrilateral have?

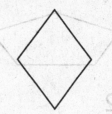

  ○ 2   ○ 4
  ○ 5   ○ 8

4. Kay draws a house. What is the shape of Kay's drawing?

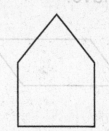

  ○ triangle
  ○ quadrilateral
  ○ pentagon
  ○ hexagon

5. How many sides and vertices does a rectangle have?

_____ sides

_____ vertices

1. How many angles does the shape have?

- ○ 2
- ○ 3
- ○ 4
- ○ 5

2. How many angles does the shape have?

- ○ 4
- ○ 5
- ○ 6
- ○ 8

3. Tom drew a shape with only 3 angles. What kind of shape did he draw?

- ○ hexagon
- ○ quadrilateral
- ○ triangle
- ○ square

4. How many angles does the shape have?

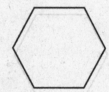

- ○ 12
- ○ 10
- ○ 8
- ○ 6

5. Draw a shape that has only four angles.
   Write the name of your shape.

_____

© Houghton Mifflin Harcourt Publishing Company

Geometry

1. Which rule matches the shapes?

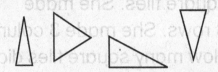

- ○ shapes with 4 angles
- ○ shapes with 3 angles
- ○ shapes with 5 angles
- ○ shapes with 4 sides

2. Which rule matches the shapes?

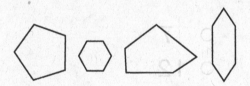

- ○ shapes with 5 sides
- ○ shapes with 6 angles
- ○ shapes with more than 4 sides
- ○ shapes with fewer than 4 angles

3. Which shape has fewer than 4 sides?

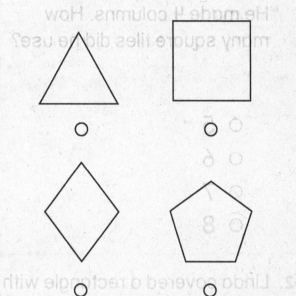

- ○   ○
- ○   ○

4. Johanna walks home from school each day. She sees that a road sign has the shape of a pentagon. How many angles does the road sign have?

- ○ 3
- ○ 4
- ○ 5
- ○ 6

5. Draw a shape that has fewer than 4 angles. Name your shape.

_____

1. Rick covered a rectangle with square tiles. He made 2 rows. He made 4 columns. How many square tiles did he use?

   ○ 5
   ○ 6
   ○ 7
   ○ 8

2. Linda covered a rectangle with square tiles. She made 5 rows. She made 1 column. How many square tiles did she use?

   ○ 10
   ○ 6
   ○ 5
   ○ 4

3. Maria covered a rectangle with square tiles. She made 3 rows. She made 3 columns. How many square tiles did she use?

   ○ 9
   ○ 8
   ○ 6
   ○ 3

4. Jeff covered a rectangle with square tiles. He made 4 rows. He made 3 columns. How many square tiles did he use?

   ○ 7
   ○ 12
   ○ 14
   ○ 16

5. Trace around the square tiles. Write how many.

Number of rows: _____

Number of columns: _____

Total: _____ square tiles

© Houghton Mifflin Harcourt Publishing Company

Geometry

1. Which whole has been divided into thirds?

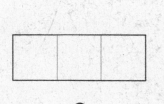 

○　　　　　　○

 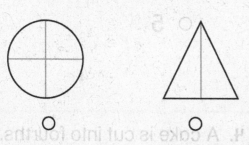

○　　　　　　○

2. Which whole has been divided into halves?

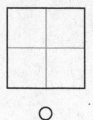 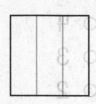

○　　　　　　○

 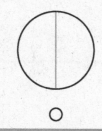

○　　　　　　○

3. Which whole has been divided into fourths?

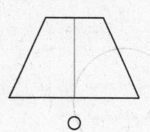 

○　　　　　　○

○　　　　　　○

4. Which shape is **not** divided into equal parts?

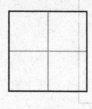

○　　　　　　○

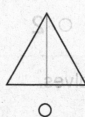 

○　　　　　　○

5. Write how many equal parts are in the whole. Write **halves**, **thirds**, or **fourths** to name the equal parts.

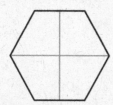 _____ equal parts

_____

Geometry

1. Alan divides a circle into thirds. How many equal parts does he show?

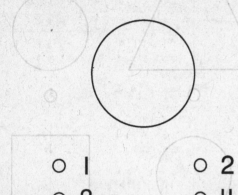

- ○ I
- ○ 3
- ○ 2
- ○ 4

2. Sue divides a rectangle into halves. How many equal parts does she show?

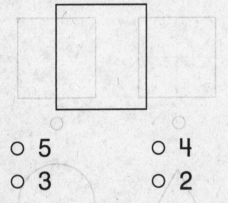

- ○ 5
- ○ 3
- ○ 4
- ○ 2

3. A sandwich is cut into thirds. How many pieces of sandwich are there?

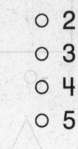

- ○ 2
- ○ 3
- ○ 4
- ○ 5

4. A cake is cut into fourths. How many pieces of cake are there in all?

- ○ 4
- ○ 3
- ○ 2
- ○ I

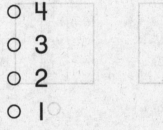

5. Draw to show halves.

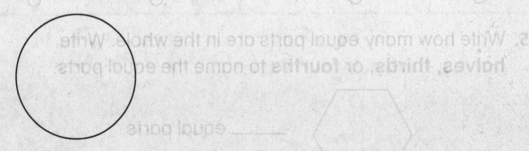

Geometry

1. How much of the shape is shaded?

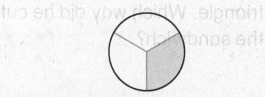

- ○ a whole
- ○ a fourth
- ○ a third
- ○ a half

3. How much of the shape is shaded?

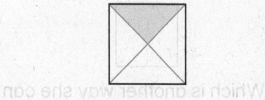

- ○ a half
- ○ a third
- ○ a fourth
- ○ a whole

2. Which of these has a half of the shape shaded?

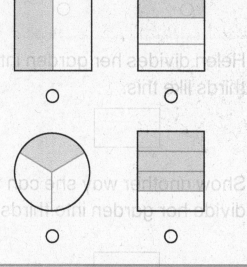

4. Which of these has a third of the shape shaded?

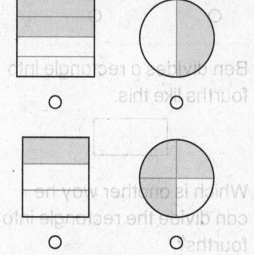

5. Draw to show fourths. Color a fourth of the shape.

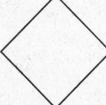

Geometry

1. Dana divides a square into halves like this.

Which is another way she can divide the square into halves?

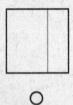

○   ○

   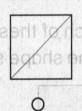

○   ○

2. Ben divides a rectangle into fourths like this.

Which is another way he can divide the rectangle into fourths?

○   ○

○   ○

3. Mr. Jones cut a sandwich into fourths. Each piece is a triangle. Which way did he cut the sandwich?

   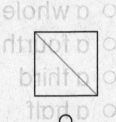

○   ○

○   ○

4. Helen divides her garden into thirds like this.

Show another way she can divide her garden into thirds.

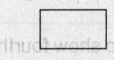

Geometry

Lesson 1
CC.2.OA.1

1. Eli has 13 marbles. Amber has 6 marbles. How many more marbles does Eli have than Amber?

13	
6	

- ● 7
- ○ 8
- ○ 10
- ○ 19

3. Julian has 14 grapes. He gives 5 grapes to Lindsay. How many grapes does Julian have left?

___	5

14

- ○ 19
- ○ 11
- ○ 10
- ● 9

2. There were 8 ants on a rock. Some more ants joined them. Then there were 13 ants on the rock. How many ants joined them?

- ○ 4
- ● 5
- ○ 13
- ○ 22

4. Sarah had 6 books. Her grandmother gave her 5 more books. How many books does Sarah have now?

- ○ 1
- ○ 10
- ● 11
- ○ 13

5. Jared has 15 red cubes. He has 7 blue cubes. How many more red cubes than blue cubes does he have? Complete the bar model.

15	
7	8

___8___ more red cubes

Operations and Algebraic Thinking   1

Lesson 2
CC.2.OA.1

1. There are 14 bees in an apple tree. There are 9 bees in a pear tree. How many more bees are in the apple tree than in the pear tree?

Which number sentence could you use to solve the problem?

- ○ 9 + 14 = ▓
- ● ▓ + 9 = 14
- ○ 9 = ▓ + 14
- ○ 14 = 9 − ▓

3. Lenny had 16 toy cars. He gave some cars to his sister. Now he has 9 cars. Which number sentence shows how many cars he gave to his sister?

- ● 16 − 9 = 7
- ○ 9 − 2 = 7
- ○ 16 − 6 = 10
- ○ 16 + 2 = 18

2. There are 11 children at the park. Then 5 children go home. Which number sentence shows how many children are still at the park?

- ○ 8 − 4 = 4
- ● 11 − 5 = 6
- ○ 11 + 5 = 16
- ○ 11 + 6 = 17

4. Write a number sentence for the problem. Use a ▓ for the missing number. Then solve.

Ann read 4 pages of a book. Then she read 8 more pages. How many pages did she read altogether?

4 + 8 = ▓

___12___ pages

Operations and Algebraic Thinking

2

Lesson 3
CC.2.OA.1

1. James and Flora have 38 markers in all. Flora has 16 markers. How many markers does James have?

- ● 22   ○ 54
- ○ 44   ○ 62

3. Miles puts 52 stickers in his notebook. Julie puts 29 stickers in her notebook. How many stickers do Miles and Julie put in their notebook in all?

- ○ 23   ● 81
- ○ 71   ○ 94

2. A pet store has two fish tanks. There are 48 fish in one tank and 23 fish in the other tank. How many fish are there in both tanks?

- ○ 25   ● 71
- ○ 26   ○ 72

4. There are 37 pencils in the pencil box. Ms. Marks hands out 18 of the pencils to the class. How many pencils are left in the pencil box?

- ○ 55   ○ 25
- ○ 29   ● 19

5. Label the bar model. Write a number sentence with a ▓ for the missing number. Solve.

Tom has 23 red pens and 38 black pens how man pens does Tom have?

23	38

61

23 + 38 = ▓

___61___ pens

Operations and Algebraic Thinking   3

Lesson 4
CC.2.OA.1

1. Gina scores 26 points in the game. Eric scores 31 points. Which number sentence can be used to find how many they score in all?

- ○ 26 + ▓ = 31
- ○ 31 + ▓ = 55
- ● 26 + 31 = ▓
- ○ 31 + 62 = ▓

3. Tim and Liz collect stamps. Tim has 93 stamps. Liz has 32 stamps. How many stamps do Tim and Liz have in all?

- ● 125   ○ 115
- ○ 120   ○ 105

2. On a hike, Sierra sees 42 frogs and 27 turtles. Which number sentence can be used to find how many frogs and turtles Sierra sees in all?

- ○ ▓ + 24 = 27
- ● 42 + 27 = ▓
- ○ 42 + 72 = ▓
- ○ 27 + ▓ = 42

4. Amber collects 49 pebbles at the beach. Meg collects 44 pebbles at the beach. How many pebbles do they collect in all?

- ○ 103
- ● 93
- ○ 83
- ○ 5

5. Write a number sentence for the problem. Use a ▓ for the missing number. Then solve.

63 people ride on the bus. 37 of them are adults and the rest are children. How many children are on the bus?

Number sentences may vary. Possible number sentence is given.

37 + ▓ = 63

___26___ children

Operations and Algebraic Thinking

4

© Houghton Mifflin Harcourt Publishing Company

Lesson 5
CC.2.OA.1

1. Mrs. Dobbs has 38 stickers. She gives away 12 stickers. Which number sentence shows how many stickers she has left?

____	____

○ $26 - 12 = 14$
○ $12 + 26 = 38$
● $38 - 12 = 26$
○ $12 - 6 = 6$

2. Which bar model shows the number sentence?

$$22 - 8 = 14$$

14	8
14
○

14	8
22
●

22	14
8
○

22	8
14
○

3. Alison makes 54 cookies. She gives away 32 cookies. Which number sentence shows how many cookies she has left?

____	____

○ $54 + 32 = 86$
○ $32 + 50 = 82$
○ $32 - 12 = 20$
● $54 - 32 = 22$

4. Larry had 46 carrots. Rabbits ate 27 carrots. How many carrots does he have left? Label the bar model. Write a number sentence with a ▓ for the missing number. Solve.

27	19
46

Possible answer: 46 − 27 =

_____ 19 carrots

© Houghton Mifflin Harcourt Publishing Company

Lesson 6
CC.2.OA.1

1. There were 27 children in a classroom. Then 18 children went outside. Which number sentence can be used to find how many children are in the classroom now?

○ $27 + 18 = $ ▓
○ $18 - 27 = $ ▓
○ $45 - 27 = $ ▓
● $27 - 18 = $ ▓

2. Ms. Clark baked some cookies. She gave 25 cookies to her friends. Now she has 7 cookies. Which number sentence can be used to find how many cookies she baked?

○ ▓ $+ 25 = 7$
● ▓ $- 25 = 7$
○ ▓ $+ 7 = 25$
○ ▓ $- 25 = 32$

3. Tom had 45 marbles. He gave 31 marbles to his sister. Which number sentence can be used to find how many marbles Tom has now?

● $45 - 31 = $ ▓
○ $31 - 45 = $ ▓
○ $45 + 31 = $ ▓
○ $76 - 31 = $ ▓

4. There were 36 apples on a tree. Some apples fell down. Now there are 11 apples on the tree. Which number sentence can be used to find how many apples fell down?

○ $36 + $ ▓ $= 11$
○ $11 - $ ▓ $= 36$
● $36 - $ ▓ $= 11$
○ $25 - $ ▓ $= 11$

5. Write a problem for the number sentence

$30 - $ ▓ $= 14$.

Possible answer: Laura had 30 dolls. She gave some away.

Now she has 14 dolls. How many dolls did she give away?

© Houghton Mifflin Harcourt Publishing Company

Lesson 7
CC.2.OA.1

1. There were 53 people in line at the movies. Then 17 people left the line. Later, 22 more people left. How many people are in line now?

○ 4   ○ 24
● 14   ○ 58

2. Molly has 39 coins in her collection. Her sister has 26 coins. How many more coins are needed so they will have 85 coins in all?

● 20   ○ 30
○ 21   ○ 65

3. Jack counted 48 ants on one log and 33 ants on another log. Some ants left. Then there were 54 ants in all. How many ants left?

○ 17   ● 27
○ 21   ○ 81

4. There were 24 ducks on a pond. Then 27 more ducks came to the pond. Later, 14 ducks flew away. How many ducks are on the pond now?

○ 51   ○ 27
● 37   ○ 21

5. Mr. Lane drove 42 miles. Then he drove 35 miles. He plans to drive 87 miles in all. How much farther does he need to drive? Draw bar models to help you solve the problem.

Check children's work.

_____ 10 miles

© Houghton Mifflin Harcourt Publishing Company

Lesson 8
CC.2.OA.2

1. Which doubles fact could you use to find the sum?

$4 + 5 = $

○ $3 + 3 = 6$
○ $4 + 6 = 10$
● $5 + 5 = 10$
○ $6 + 6 = 12$

2. Which doubles fact could you use to find the sum?

$9 + 8 = $

● $8 + 8 = 16$
○ $7 + 7 = 14$
○ $9 + 1 = 10$
○ $10 + 10 = 20$

3. What is the sum?

$7 + 6 = $ _____

○ 11
○ 12
● 13
○ 14

4. Maggie picked 3 apples. Lisa picked 4 apples. How many apples did they pick in all?

○ 6
● 7
○ 8
○ 9

5. Kevin has 5 marbles. Jen has 6 marbles. How many marbles do they have in all?

Write a doubles fact you can use to find the sum. Then write the sum.

Possible answer: 5 + 5 = 10;

11 marbles

© Houghton Mifflin Harcourt Publishing Company

---

1. What is the sum for both number sentences?

   6 + 1 = _____

   1 + 6 = _____

   ○ 4
   ○ 5
   ○ 6
   ● 7

2. What is the sum?

   8 + 7 = _____

   ○ 13
   ○ 14
   ● 15
   ○ 16

3. Which of the following has the same sum?

   2 + 9 = ?

   ○ 8 + 2
   ● 9 + 2
   ○ 2 + 10
   ○ 3 + 9

4. Marco had 6 stamps. His mother gave him 3 more stamps. How many stamps does Marco have now?

   ○ 7
   ○ 8
   ● 9
   ○ 10

5. Explain why 5 + 4 and 4 + 5 have the same sum.

Possible answer: Changing the order of the addends does not change the sum.

1. How could you break apart the 7 to make a ten?

   6 + 7

   6 + _____ + _____

   ○ 2 + 5
   ● 4 + 3
   ○ 5 + 2
   ○ 1 + 6

2. What is the sum?

   9 + 5 = _____

   ○ 11
   ○ 12
   ○ 13
   ● 14

3. How could you break apart the 9 to make a ten?

   8 + 9

   8 + _____ + _____

   ○ 7 + 2
   ○ 4 + 5
   ● 2 + 7
   ○ 3 + 6

4. What is the sum?

   4 + 8 = _____

   ○ 2
   ● 12
   ○ 13
   ○ 16

5. Draw to show how you can make a ten to find the sum. Write the sum.

   Check children's drawings.

   5 + 7 = __12__

   10 + __2__ = __12__

1. What is the sum?

   2 + 4 + 8 = _____

   ○ 12
   ● 14
   ○ 15
   ○ 16

2. What is the sum?

   4
   3
   + 6

   ● 13
   ○ 10
   ○ 9
   ○ 7

3. What is the sum?

   4
   5
   + 7

   ○ 9
   ○ 11
   ● 16
   ○ 17

4. Ava grows 3 red flowers, 4 yellow flowers, and 4 purple flowers in her garden. How many flowers does Ava grow in all?

   ○ 7
   ○ 8
   ○ 10
   ● 11

5. Solve two ways. Circle the two addends you add first.

   Circled addends will vary.

   3 + 7 + 5 = __15__   3 + 7 + 5 = __15__

1. What is the difference for the related subtraction fact?

   9 + 6 = 15

   15 − 9 = _____

   ○ 3
   ○ 4
   ○ 5
   ● 6

2. What is the sum for the related addition fact?

   12 − 7 = 5

   5 + 7 = _____

   ○ 11
   ● 12
   ○ 13
   ○ 14

3. Which shows a related addition fact?

   13 − 6 = 7

   ● 6 + 7 = 13
   ○ 7 + 13 = 20
   ○ 7 − 6 = 1
   ○ 13 + 6 = 19

4. There are 11 brown birds and 5 red birds in a tree. How many more brown birds than red birds are there?

   ○ 5
   ● 6
   ○ 7
   ○ 9

5. Write the sum and the difference for the related facts.

   8 + 8 = __16__

   16 − 8 = __8__

Name _____

Lesson 13
CC.2.OA.2

I. What is the difference?

$15 - 7 =$ _____

○ 7
● 8
○ 12
○ 15

3. What is the difference?

$16 - 7 =$ _____

● 9
○ 8
○ 7
○ 6

2. What is the difference?

_____ $= 13 - 9$

● 4
○ 5
○ 6
○ 7

4. Elena invited 8 friends to her party. 2 of them could not go. How many friends went to Elena's party?

○ 2
○ 4
○ 5
● 6

5. Write the difference.
Draw to show your work.

Check children's drawings.

___5___ $= 9 - 4$

Name _____

Lesson 14
CC.2.OA.2

I. Which tens fact could you use to find the difference?

$11 - 4 =$ _____
$\overset{?\quad?}{/\ \backslash}$

○ $10 - 5 = 5$
○ $10 - 4 = 6$
● $10 - 3 = 7$
○ $10 - 2 = 8$

3. Mr. Brown picked 12 plums. He gave 8 plums away. How many plums did he have left?

○ 3
● 4
○ 5
○ 6

2. Which tens fact could you use to find the difference?

$16 - 7 =$ _____
$\overset{?\quad?}{/\ \backslash}$

○ $10 - 4 = 6$
○ $10 - 3 = 7$
○ $10 - 2 = 8$
● $10 - 1 = 9$

4. Which number makes the number sentence true?

$13 - 5 = 8$

$10 -$ _____ $= 8$

● 2
○ 3
○ 4
○ 6

5. Show the tens fact you used. Write the difference.

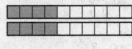

$12 - 4 =$ ___8___
$\quad\ /\ \backslash$
$\quad 2 \quad 2$

$10 -$ ___2___ $=$ ___8___

Name _____

Lesson 15
CC.2.OA.3

I. The Morris family has an even number of dogs and an odd number of cats. Which could be the number of pets in the Morris family?

○ I dog and 2 cats
○ I dog and 3 cats
○ 2 dogs and 2 cats
● 2 dogs and I cat

2. Elsa shades a pair of ten frames to show an even number. Which could be Elsa's ten frames?

○
○
●
○

3. Shade this pair of ten frames to show an even number greater than 15. Explain how you know the number is even.

Answers will vary. Check that children's numbers match the explanations.

_____

Name _____

Lesson 16
CC.2.OA.3

I. The frames show two groups for 8. Which addition sentence shows the groups?

○ $1 + 7 = 8$
○ $2 + 6 = 8$
○ $3 + 5 = 8$
● $4 + 4 = 8$

2. Mary and Ana each have the same number of stickers. They have 10 stickers altogether. Which addition sentence shows the number of stickers Mary and Ana each have?

○ $4 + 6 = 10$
● $5 + 5 = 10$
○ $3 + 7 = 10$
○ $2 + 8 = 10$

3. Draw to show that 12 is an even number.

Children's drawings may vary.

1. Ms. Green put 4 stamps on each card. How many stamps will she put on 5 cards?

- ● 20
- ○ 16
- ○ 9
- ○ 8

3. Eric puts his dimes in 5 rows. He puts 3 dimes in each row. How many dimes does he have in all?

- ○ 5
- ○ 8
- ○ 12
- ● 15

2. Gina has 4 mice cages. There are 4 mice in each cage. How many mice does Gina have?

- ○ 8
- ○ 10
- ○ 12
- ● 16

4. Rachel puts 4 pencils in each box. How many pencils will she put in 3 boxes?

- ○ 16
- ● 12
- ○ 7
- ○ 4

5. Rob puts 3 counters in each row. How many counters in all does he put in 4 rows? Draw to show your work.

Check children's work.

___12___ counters

---

1. Which could you use to find the number of squares?

- ● 5 + 5 + 5 + 5 = ____
- ○ 5 + 5 + 5 = ____
- ○ 4 + 4 + 4 = ____
- ○ 4 + 4 + 4 + 4 = ____

3. Which could you use to find the number of circles?

- ○ 3 + 3 + 3 = ____
- ○ 3 + 3 + 3 + 3 = ____
- ● 5 + 5 + 5 = ____
- ○ 5 + 5 + 5 + 5 = ____

2. Some children sat in 2 rows. There were 3 children in each row. How many children were there in all?

- ○ 1
- ○ 2
- ○ 5
- ● 6

4. Mr. Henry has 4 rows of trees. There are 2 trees in each row. How many trees does he have in all?

- ○ 10
- ● 8
- ○ 6
- ○ 2

5. Find the number of shapes in each row. Complete the addition sentence to find the total.

3 rows of _3_

_3_ + _3_ + _3_ = _9_

---

1. Which has the same value as 12 tens?

- ○ 2 tens
- ○ 1 hundred 1 ten
- ● 1 hundred 2 tens
- ○ 2 hundreds

3. Which shows how many hundreds and tens?

- ● 1 hundred 3 tens
- ○ 1 hundred 4 tens
- ○ 1 hundred 8 tens
- ○ 2 hundreds 3 tens

2. Which has the same value as 14 tens?

- ○ 4 tens
- ○ 40 tens
- ● 1 hundred 4 tens
- ○ 1 hundred 14 tens

4. Which shows how many hundreds and tens?

- ○ 1 hundred 1 ten
- ● 1 hundred 5 tens
- ○ 5 hundreds 1 ten
- ○ 5 hundreds 5 tens

5. A number is made with 17 tens. Write the number in two different ways.

__1__ hundred __7__ tens

_170_

---

1. Kelly uses blocks to make the number 102. Which shows 102?

3. Which chart shows how many hundreds, tens, and ones are in 241?

	Hundreds	Tens	Ones
○	4	2	1

	Hundreds	Tens	Ones
●	2	4	1

	Hundreds	Tens	Ones
○	1	4	2

	Hundreds	Tens	Ones
○	2	1	4

2. What number is shown with these blocks?

- ○ 167
- ○ 252
- ● 257
- ○ 262

4. Which chart shows how many hundreds, tens, and ones are in 423?

	Hundreds	Tens	Ones
●	4	2	3

	Hundreds	Tens	Ones
○	4	3	2

	Hundreds	Tens	Ones
○	2	4	3

	Hundreds	Tens	Ones
○	3	4	2

5. A model for a number has 2 hundreds blocks, 3 tens blocks, and no ones blocks. Complete the chart. Write the number.

Hundreds	Tens	Ones
2	3	0

_230_

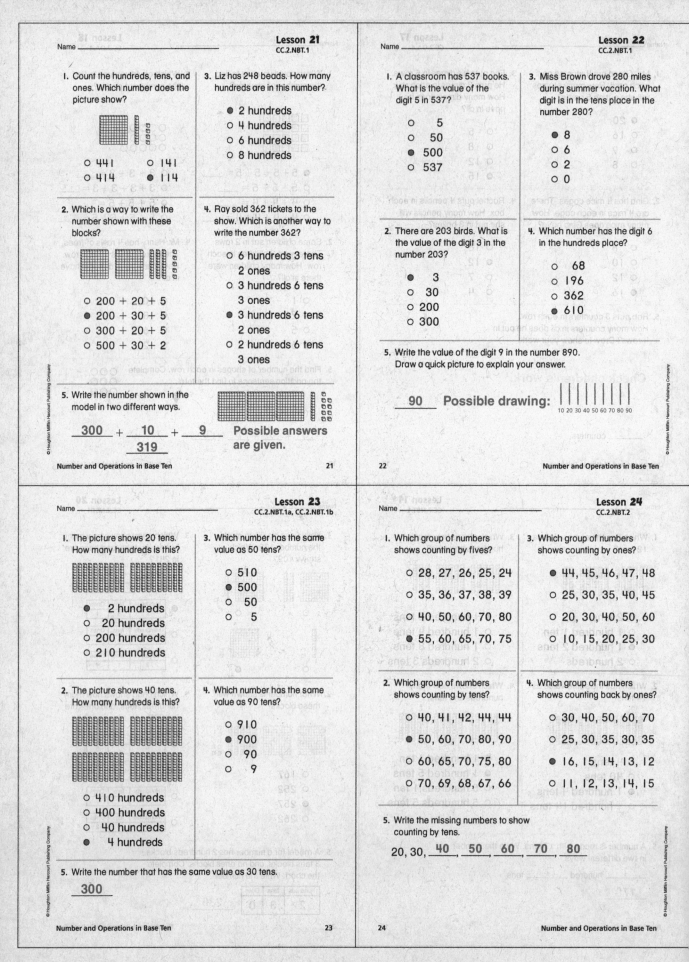

Lesson 21
CC.2.NBT.1

Name _____

1. Count the hundreds, tens, and ones. Which number does the picture show?

○ 441   ○ 141
○ 414   ● 114

2. Which is a way to write the number shown with these blocks?

○ 200 + 20 + 5
● 200 + 30 + 5
○ 300 + 20 + 5
○ 500 + 30 + 2

3. Liz has 248 beads. How many hundreds are in this number?

● 2 hundreds
○ 4 hundreds
○ 6 hundreds
○ 8 hundreds

4. Ray sold 362 tickets to the show. Which is another way to write the number 362?

○ 6 hundreds 3 tens 2 ones
○ 3 hundreds 6 tens 3 ones
● 3 hundreds 6 tens 2 ones
○ 2 hundreds 6 tens 3 ones

5. Write the number shown in the model in two different ways.

__300__ + __10__ + __9__
__319__

Possible answers are given.

Number and Operations in Base Ten   21

Lesson 22
CC.2.NBT.1

Name _____

1. A classroom has 537 books. What is the value of the digit 5 in 537?

○ 5
○ 50
● 500
○ 537

2. There are 203 birds. What is the value of the digit 3 in the number 203?

● 3
○ 30
○ 200
○ 300

3. Miss Brown drove 280 miles during summer vacation. What digit is in the tens place in the number 280?

● 8
○ 6
○ 2
○ 0

4. Which number has the digit 6 in the hundreds place?

○ 68
○ 196
○ 362
● 610

5. Write the value of the digit 9 in the number 890. Draw a quick picture to explain your answer.

__90__   **Possible drawing:**
10 20 30 40 50 60 70 80 90

22   Number and Operations in Base Ten

Lesson 23
CC.2.NBT.1a, CC.2.NBT.1b

Name _____

1. The picture shows 20 tens. How many hundreds is this?

● 2 hundreds
○ 20 hundreds
○ 200 hundreds
○ 210 hundreds

2. The picture shows 40 tens. How many hundreds is this?

○ 410 hundreds
○ 400 hundreds
○ 40 hundreds
● 4 hundreds

3. Which number has the same value as 50 tens?

○ 510
● 500
○ 50
○ 5

4. Which number has the same value as 90 tens?

○ 910
● 900
○ 90
○ 9

5. Write the number that has the same value as 30 tens.

__300__

Number and Operations in Base Ten   23

Lesson 24
CC.2.NBT.2

Name _____

1. Which group of numbers shows counting by fives?

○ 28, 27, 26, 25, 24
○ 35, 36, 37, 38, 39
○ 40, 50, 60, 70, 80
● 55, 60, 65, 70, 75

2. Which group of numbers shows counting by tens?

○ 40, 41, 42, 44, 44
● 50, 60, 70, 80, 90
○ 60, 65, 70, 75, 80
○ 70, 69, 68, 67, 66

3. Which group of numbers shows counting by ones?

● 44, 45, 46, 47, 48
○ 25, 30, 35, 40, 45
○ 20, 30, 40, 50, 60
○ 10, 15, 20, 25, 30

4. Which group of numbers shows counting back by ones?

○ 30, 40, 50, 60, 70
○ 25, 30, 35, 30, 35
● 16, 15, 14, 13, 12
○ 11, 12, 13, 14, 15

5. Write the missing numbers to show counting by tens.

20, 30, __40__, __50__, __60__, __70__, __80__

24   Number and Operations in Base Ten

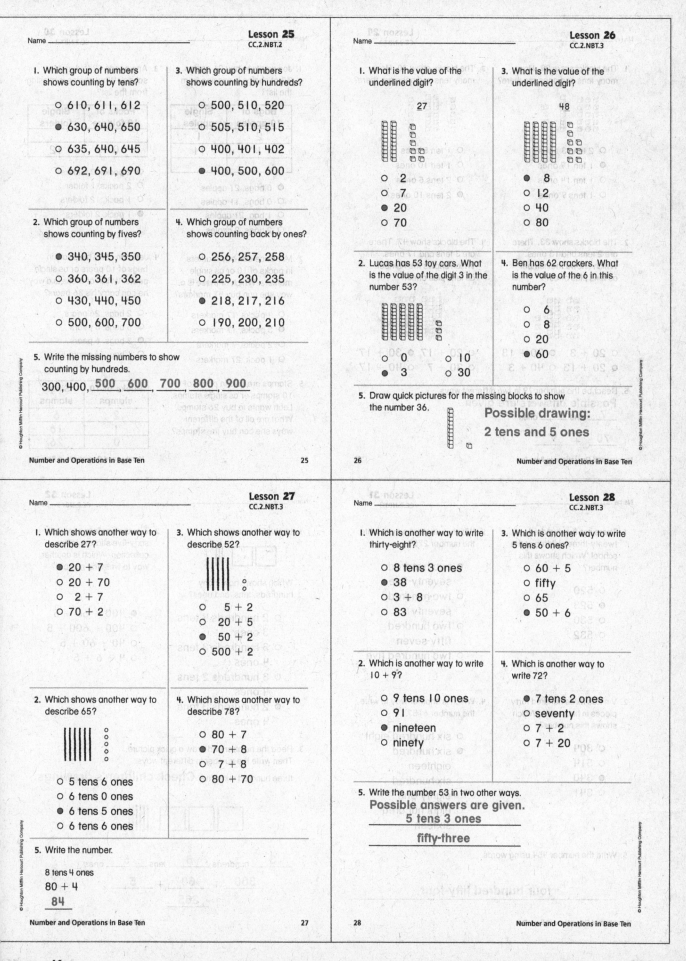

Lesson 25
CC.2.NBT.2

1. Which group of numbers shows counting by tens?

- ○ 610, 611, 612
- ● 630, 640, 650
- ○ 635, 640, 645
- ○ 692, 691, 690

2. Which group of numbers shows counting by fives?

- ● 340, 345, 350
- ○ 360, 361, 362
- ○ 430, 440, 450
- ○ 500, 600, 700

3. Which group of numbers shows counting by hundreds?

- ○ 500, 510, 520
- ○ 505, 510, 515
- ○ 400, 401, 402
- ● 400, 500, 600

4. Which group of numbers shows counting back by ones?

- ○ 256, 257, 258
- ○ 225, 230, 235
- ● 218, 217, 216
- ○ 190, 200, 210

5. Write the missing numbers to show counting by hundreds.

300, 400, __500__, __600__, __700__, __800__, __900__

Lesson 26
CC.2.NBT.3

1. What is the value of the underlined digit?

2̲7

- ○ 2
- ○ 7
- ● 20
- ○ 70

2. Lucas has 53 toy cars. What is the value of the digit 3 in the number 53?

- ○ 0   ○ 10
- ● 3   ○ 30

3. What is the value of the underlined digit?

4̲8

- ● 8
- ○ 12
- ○ 40
- ○ 80

4. Ben has 62 crackers. What is the value of the 6 in this number?

- ○ 6
- ○ 8
- ○ 20
- ● 60

5. Draw quick pictures for the missing blocks to show the number 36.

Possible drawing:
2 tens and 5 ones

Lesson 27
CC.2.NBT.3

1. Which shows another way to describe 27?

- ● 20 + 7
- ○ 20 + 70
- ○ 2 + 7
- ○ 70 + 2

2. Which shows another way to describe 65?

- ○ 5 tens 6 ones
- ○ 6 tens 0 ones
- ● 6 tens 5 ones
- ○ 6 tens 6 ones

3. Which shows another way to describe 52?

- ○ 5 + 2
- ○ 20 + 5
- ● 50 + 2
- ○ 500 + 2

4. Which shows another way to describe 78?

- ○ 80 + 7
- ● 70 + 8
- ○ 7 + 8
- ○ 80 + 70

5. Write the number.

8 tens 4 ones
80 + 4
__84__

Lesson 28
CC.2.NBT.3

1. Which is another way to write thirty-eight?

- ○ 8 tens 3 ones
- ● 38
- ○ 3 + 8
- ○ 83

2. Which is another way to write 10 + 9?

- ○ 9 tens 10 ones
- ○ 91
- ● nineteen
- ○ ninety

3. Which is another way to write 5 tens 6 ones?

- ○ 60 + 5
- ○ fifty
- ○ 65
- ● 50 + 6

4. Which is another way to write 72?

- ● 7 tens 2 ones
- ○ seventy
- ○ 7 + 2
- ○ 7 + 20

5. Write the number 53 in two other ways.
Possible answers are given.

__5 tens 3 ones__

__fifty-three__

Lesson 29
CC.2.NBT.3

1. The blocks show 29. How many tens and ones are there?

   ○ 2 tens 3 ones
   ● 1 ten 19 ones
   ○ 1 ten 14 ones
   ○ 1 tens 9 ones

3. The blocks show 30. How many tens and ones are there?

   ○ 1 ten 5 ones
   ○ 1 ten 10 ones
   ○ 2 tens 5 ones
   ● 2 tens 10 ones

2. The blocks show 33. There are 2 tens and 13 ones. Which shows the number as tens plus ones?

   ○ 20 + 3   ○ 30 + 13
   ● 20 + 13   ○ 40 + 3

4. The blocks show 47. There are 3 tens and 17 ones. Which shows the number as tens plus ones?

   ○ 20 + 17   ● 30 + 17
   ○ 30 + 7   ○ 40 + 17

5. Describe the number 79 in two different ways.
   Possible answers are given.

   __7__ tens __9__ ones

   __70__ + __9__

Number and Operations in Base Ten   29

Lesson 30
CC.2.NBT.3

1. Jon wants to buy 21 apples. What choice is missing from the list?

Bags of 10 apples	Single apples
2	1
1	11

   ● 0 bags, 21 apples
   ○ 0 bags, 11 apples
   ○ 1 bag, 21 apples
   ○ 2 bags, 2 apples

3. Ann needs 12 folders for school. What choice is missing from the list?

Packs of 10 folders	Single folders
0	12

   ○ 2 packs, 0 folders
   ○ 2 packs, 1 folder
   ○ 1 pack, 12 folders
   ● 1 pack, 2 folders

2. Ms. Brice can buy markers in packs of 10 or as single markers. Which of these is a way she can buy 47 markers?

   ○ 4 packs, 17 markers
   ● 3 packs, 17 markers
   ○ 2 packs, 7 markers
   ○ 1 pack, 27 markers

4. Jeff can carry his pears in bags of 10 pears or as single pears. Which of these is a way he can carry his 36 pears?

   ○ 2 bags, 26 pears
   ○ 6 bags, 3 pears
   ● 3 bags, 6 pears
   ○ 1 bag, 16 pears

5. Stamps are sold in packs of 10 stamps or as single stamps. Leah wants to buy 26 stamps. What are all of the different ways she can buy the stamps?

Packs of 10 stamps	Single stamps
2	6
1	16
0	26

30   Number and Operations in Base Ten

Lesson 31
CC.2.NBT.3

1. There are five hundred twenty-three children at the school. Which shows this number?

   ○ 520
   ● 523
   ○ 530
   ○ 532

3. Which is another way to write the number 275?

   ● two hundred seventy-five
   ○ two hundred seventy
   ○ two hundred fifty-seven
   ○ two hundred five

2. Vin has three hundred forty pieces in his puzzle. Which shows this number?

   ○ 304
   ○ 314
   ● 340
   ○ 341

4. Which is another way to write the number 618?

   ○ six hundred eight
   ● six hundred eighteen
   ○ six hundred eighty-one
   ○ eight hundred sixteen

5. Write the number 454 using words.

   four hundred fifty-four

Number and Operations in Base Ten   31

Lesson 32
CC.2.NBT.3

1. Look at the picture.

   Which shows how many hundreds, tens, and ones?

   ○ 2 hundreds 4 tens 3 ones
   ○ 3 hundreds 3 tens 4 ones
   ○ 3 hundreds 2 tens 4 ones
   ● 2 hundreds 3 tens 4 ones

2. Claudia has four hundred sixty-five stickers in her collection. Which is another way to write the number?

   ● 400 + 60 + 5
   ○ 400 + 600 + 5
   ○ 40 + 60 + 5
   ○ 4 + 6 + 5

3. Read the number and draw a quick picture. Then write the number in different ways.

   three hundred sixty-five **Check children's drawings.**

   __3__ hundreds __6__ tens __5__ ones

   __300__ + __60__ + __5__

   __365__

32   Number and Operations in Base Ten

116

Answer Key

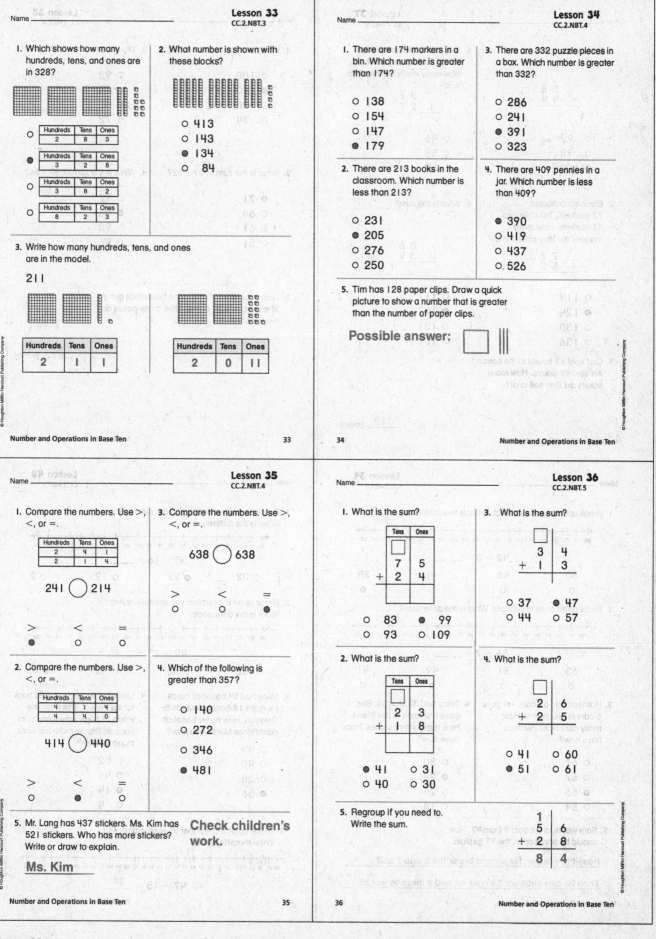

Lesson 33
CC.2.NBT.3

1. Which shows how many hundreds, tens, and ones are in 328?

○ | Hundreds | Tens | Ones |
  |---|---|---|
  | 2 | 8 | 3 |

● | Hundreds | Tens | Ones |
  |---|---|---|
  | 3 | 2 | 8 |

○ | Hundreds | Tens | Ones |
  |---|---|---|
  | 3 | 8 | 2 |

○ | Hundreds | Tens | Ones |
  |---|---|---|
  | 8 | 2 | 3 |

2. What number is shown with these blocks?

○ 413
○ 143
● 134
○ 84

3. Write how many hundreds, tens, and ones are in the model.

211

Hundreds	Tens	Ones
2	1	1

Hundreds	Tens	Ones
2	0	11

Number and Operations in Base Ten

33

Lesson 34
CC.2.NBT.4

1. There are 174 markers in a bin. Which number is greater than 174?

○ 138
○ 154
○ 147
● 179

2. There are 213 books in the classroom. Which number is less than 213?

○ 231
● 205
○ 276
○ 250

3. There are 332 puzzle pieces in a box. Which number is greater than 332?

○ 286
○ 241
● 391
○ 323

4. There are 409 pennies in a jar. Which number is less than 409?

● 390
○ 419
○ 437
○ 526

5. Tim has 128 paper clips. Draw a quick picture to show a number that is greater than the number of paper clips.

Possible answer:

34   Number and Operations in Base Ten

Lesson 35
CC.2.NBT.4

1. Compare the numbers. Use >, <, or =.

Hundreds	Tens	Ones
2	4	1
2	1	4

241 ◯ 214

> ●   < ○   = ○

2. Compare the numbers. Use >, <, or =.

Hundreds	Tens	Ones
4	1	4
4	4	0

414 ◯ 440

> ○   < ●   = ○

3. Compare the numbers. Use >, <, or =.

638 ◯ 638

> ○   < ○   = ●

4. Which of the following is greater than 357?

○ 140
○ 272
○ 346
● 481

5. Mr. Lang has 437 stickers. Ms. Kim has 521 stickers. Who has more stickers? Write or draw to explain.

Ms. Kim

Check children's work.

Number and Operations in Base Ten

35

Lesson 36
CC.2.NBT.5

1. What is the sum?

Tens	Ones
	7	5
+	2	4

○ 83   ● 99
○ 93   ○ 109

2. What is the sum?

Tens	Ones
	2	3
+	1	8

● 41   ○ 31
○ 40   ○ 30

3. What is the sum?

	3	4
+	1	3

○ 37   ● 47
○ 44   ○ 57

4. What is the sum?

	2	6
+	2	5

○ 41   ○ 60
● 51   ○ 61

5. Regroup if you need to. Write the sum.

1	
5	6
+ 2	8
8	4

36   Number and Operations in Base Ten

1. What is the sum?

$$\begin{array}{r} 5\ 8 \\ +\ 4\ 4 \\ \hline \end{array}$$

- ○ 92
- ○ 98
- ● 102
- ○ 112

2. Elizabeth collected 72 markers. Tori collected 52 markers. How many markers did they collect in all?

$$\begin{array}{r} 7\ 2 \\ +\ 5\ 2 \\ \hline \end{array}$$

- ○ 114
- ● 124
- ○ 130
- ○ 136

3. Tony found 31 shells on the beach. Andy found 27 shells. How many shells did they find in all?

$$\begin{array}{r} 3\ 1 \\ +\ 2\ 7 \\ \hline \end{array}$$

- ○ 46
- ○ 48
- ○ 54
- ● 58

4. What is the sum?

$$\begin{array}{r} 8\ 8 \\ +\ 3\ 9 \\ \hline \end{array}$$

- ○ 117
- ● 127
- ○ 131
- ○ 139

5. Curt sold 63 tickets to the concert. Art sold 49 tickets. How many tickets did they sell in all?

___112___ tickets

1. What is the sum of 34 + 56?

- ○ 100
- ● 90
- ○ 80
- ○ 74

2. What is the sum of 39 + 32?

- ● 71
- ○ 68
- ○ 61
- ○ 51

3. What is the sum of 18 + 64?

- ○ 92
- ○ 84
- ● 82
- ○ 72

4. What is the sum of 40 + 56?

- ○ 97
- ● 96
- ○ 90
- ○ 86

5. Lynn scored 23 points in the basketball game. Shelly scored 28 points. How many points did they score in all?

___51___ points

1. Break apart ones to subtract. What is the difference?

30 31 32 33 34 35 36 37 38 39 40 41 42 43 44 45 46 47 48 49 50

$$42 - 8 = \_\_\_$$

- 50 ○
- 46 ○
- 44 ○
- 34 ●

2. Break apart ones to subtract. What is the difference?

40 41 42 43 44 45 46 47 48 49 50 51 52 53 54 55 56 57 58 59 60

$$56 - 7 = \_\_\_$$

- 63 ○
- 51 ○
- 49 ●
- 41 ○

3. Harrison had 61 cars. He gave 6 cars to his brother. How many cars does Harrison have now?

- ○ 67
- ○ 57
- ● 55
- ○ 54

4. Tracy had 33 stamps. She gave 5 stamps to her friend. How many stamps does Tracy have now?

- ○ 30
- ● 28
- ○ 25
- ○ 18

5. Sam wants to subtract 9 from 47. How should he break apart the 9? Explain.

Possible answer: He should break the 9 into 7 and 2.

Then he can subtract 7 to get 40, and 2 more to get 38.

1. Break apart the number you are subtracting. What is the difference?

20 21 22 23 24 25 26 27 28 29 30 31 32 33 34 35 36 37 38 39 40

$$38 - 16 = \_\_\_$$

- ○ 32
- ● 22
- ○ 12
- ○ 2

2. Break apart the number you are subtracting. What is the difference?

30 31 32 33 34 35 36 37 38 39 40 41 42 43 44 45 46 47 48 49 50

$$49 - 13 = \_\_\_$$

- ○ 62
- ○ 46
- ○ 42
- ● 36

3. Miles had 54 baseball cards. He gave 18 baseball cards to Greyson. How many baseball cards does Miles have now?

- ○ 44
- ○ 40
- ○ 38
- ● 36

4. Last week Brooke made 28 bags for the festival. This week she made 14 bags. How many more bags did Brooke make last week than this week?

- ○ 52
- ○ 44
- ● 14
- ○ 4

5. Break apart the number you are subtracting. Write the difference.

20 21 22 23 24 25 26 27 28 29 30 31 32 33 34 35 36 37 38 39 40 41 42 43 44 45 46 47 48 49 50

$$47 - 15 = \_\_32\_\_$$

1. What is the difference?

Tens	Ones
□	□
4	7
− 1	6

○ 21   ○ 30
○ 29   ● 31

3. What is the difference?

Tens	Ones
□	□
6	1
− 2	8

○ 43   ○ 32
● 33   ○ 23

2. What is the difference?

Tens	Ones
□	□
2	4
− 1	7

○ 17   ● 7
○ 8   ○ 5

4. Miguel read 36 pages today. He read 15 pages yesterday. How many more pages did he read today than yesterday?

● 21   ○ 31
○ 23   ○ 51

5. Peter is subtracting 24 from 55. Explain why he does not need to regroup 1 ten as 10 ones.

Possible answer: There are enough ones to subtract

4 from 5. 5 − 4 = 1. So he does not need to regroup.

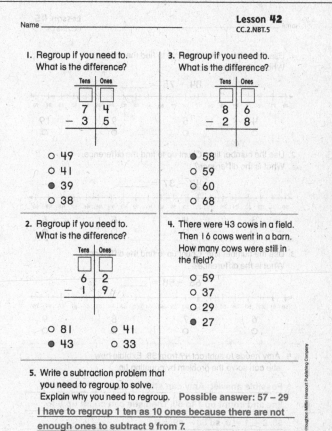

1. Regroup if you need to. What is the difference?

Tens	Ones
□	□
7	4
− 3	5

○ 49
○ 41
● 39
○ 38

3. Regroup if you need to. What is the difference?

Tens	Ones
□	□
8	6
− 2	8

● 58
○ 59
○ 60
○ 68

2. Regroup if you need to. What is the difference?

Tens	Ones
□	□
6	2
− 1	9

○ 81   ○ 41
● 43   ○ 33

4. There were 43 cows in a field. Then 16 cows went in a barn. How many cows were still in the field?

○ 59
○ 37
○ 29
● 27

5. Write a subtraction problem that you need to regroup to solve. Explain why you need to regroup.   Possible answer: 57 − 29

I have to regroup 1 ten as 10 ones because there are not

enough ones to subtract 9 from 7.

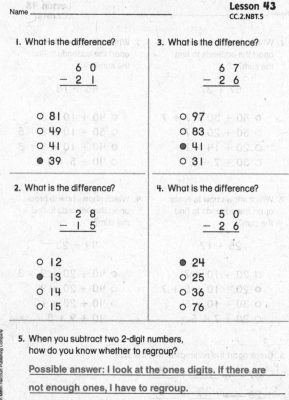

1. What is the difference?

6 0
− 2 1

○ 81
○ 49
○ 41
● 39

3. What is the difference?

6 7
− 2 6

○ 97
○ 83
● 41
○ 31

2. What is the difference?

2 8
− 1 5

○ 12
● 13
○ 14
○ 15

4. What is the difference?

5 0
− 2 6

● 24
○ 25
○ 36
○ 76

5. When you subtract two 2-digit numbers, how do you know whether to regroup?

Possible answer: I look at the ones digits. If there are

not enough ones, I have to regroup.

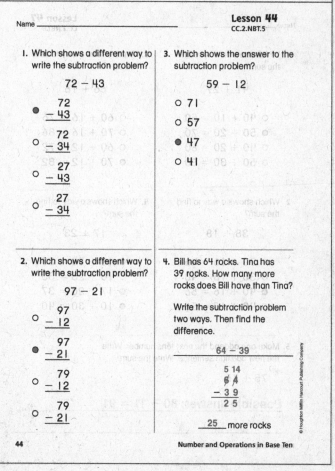

1. Which shows a different way to write the subtraction problem?

72 − 43

● 72 / − 43
○ 72 / − 34
○ 27 / − 43
○ 27 / − 34

3. Which shows the answer to the subtraction problem?

59 − 12

○ 71
○ 57
● 47
○ 41

2. Which shows a different way to write the subtraction problem?

97 − 21

○ 97 / − 12
● 97 / − 21
○ 79 / − 12
○ 79 / − 21

4. Bill has 64 rocks. Tina has 39 rocks. How many more rocks does Bill have than Tina?

Write the subtraction problem two ways. Then find the difference.

64 − 39

5 14
6 4
− 3 9
2 5

25 more rocks

Answer Key

119

Name _____

Lesson 45
CC.2.NBT.5

1. Use the number line. Count up to find the difference.
What is the difference?

$$84 - 75 = \underline{}$$

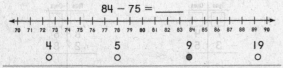

70 71 72 73 74 75 76 77 78 79 80 81 82 83 84 85 86 87 88 89 90

4	5	9	19
○	○	●	○

2. Use the number line. Count up to find the difference.
What is the difference?

$$43 - 37 = \underline{}$$

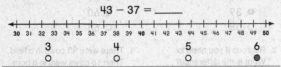

30 31 32 33 34 35 36 37 38 39 40 41 42 43 44 45 46 47 48 49 50

3	4	5	6
○	○	○	●

3. Use the number line. Count up to find the difference.
What is the difference?

$$66 - 58 = \underline{}$$

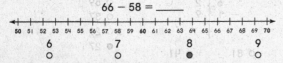

50 51 52 53 54 55 56 57 58 59 60 61 62 63 64 65 66 67 68 69 70

6	7	8	9
○	○	●	○

4. Amy needs to subtract 49 from 58. Explain how
she can solve the problem by counting up.

Possible answer: Amy can start at 49 on the number

line and count up 1 to 50. Then she can count up 8 to

58. 8 + 1 = 9, so 58 − 49 = 9.

Number and Operations in Base Ten   45

Name _____

Lesson 46
CC.2.NBT.6

1. Break apart ones to make
a ten. What is the sum?

$$17 + 8 = \underline{}$$

- ○ 13
- ○ 15
- ○ 24
- ● 25

3. Break apart ones to make
a ten. What is the sum?

$$89 + 5 = \underline{}$$

- ○ 104
- ● 94
- ○ 84
- ○ 83

2. Break apart ones to make a
ten. What is the sum?

$$57 + 4 = \underline{}$$

- ○ 31
- ○ 41
- ○ 51
- ● 61

4. Break apart ones to make
a ten. What is the sum?

$$32 + 9 = \underline{}$$

- ● 41
- ○ 40
- ○ 31
- ○ 30

5. Break apart ones to make a ten. Write the sum.

$$27 + 7 = \underline{\ 34\ }$$

46   Number and Operations in Base Ten

Name _____

Lesson 47
CC.2.NBT.6

1. Which shows a way to find
the sum?

$$41 + 29$$

- ○ $40 + 10 = 50$
- ● $50 + 20 = 70$
- ○ $40 + 20 = 60$
- ○ $50 + 30 = 80$

3. Which shows a way to find
the sum?

$$66 + 16$$

- ○ $60 + 16 = 76$
- ○ $70 + 16 = 86$
- ○ $60 + 12 = 72$
- ● $70 + 12 = 82$

2. Which shows a way to find
the sum?

$$38 + 18$$

- ○ $30 + 16 = 46$
- ○ $30 + 18 = 48$
- ● $40 + 16 = 56$
- ○ $40 + 18 = 58$

4. Which shows a way to find
the sum?

$$17 + 23$$

- ○ $10 + 20 = 30$
- ○ $10 + 23 = 33$
- ○ $17 + 20 = 37$
- ● $10 + 30 = 40$

5. Make one addend the next tens number. Write
the new addition sentence. Write the sum.

$$75 + 16$$

Possible answer: $80 + 11 = 91$

Number and Operations in Base Ten   47

Name _____

Lesson 48
CC.2.NBT.6

1. Which shows how to break
apart the addends to find
the sum?

$$57 + 37$$

- ● $50 + 30 + 7 + 7$
- ○ $50 + 20 + 7$
- ○ $20 + 14 + 7$
- ○ $30 + 7 + 7$

3. Which shows how to break
apart the addends to find
the sum?

$$45 + 18$$

- ○ $40 + 10 + 5$
- ○ $50 + 10 + 8 + 5$
- ● $40 + 10 + 5 + 8$
- ○ $40 + 5 + 8$

2. Which shows how to break
apart the addends to find
the sum?

$$25 + 17$$

- ○ $20 + 10 + 7$
- ● $20 + 10 + 5 + 7$
- ○ $30 + 10 + 5$
- ○ $20 + 7 + 5$

4. Which shows how to break
apart the addends to find
the sum?

$$49 + 23$$

- ● $40 + 20 + 9 + 3$
- ○ $40 + 20 + 9$
- ○ $40 + 20 + 10$
- ○ $40 + 9 + 3$

5. Break apart the addends to find the sum.

$$67 \longrightarrow \underline{\ 60\ } + \underline{\ 7\ }$$
$$+ 28 \longrightarrow \underline{\ 20\ } + \underline{\ 8\ }$$
$$\underline{\ 80\ } + \underline{\ 15\ } = \underline{\ 95\ }$$

48   Number and Operations in Base Ten

120

Answer Ke

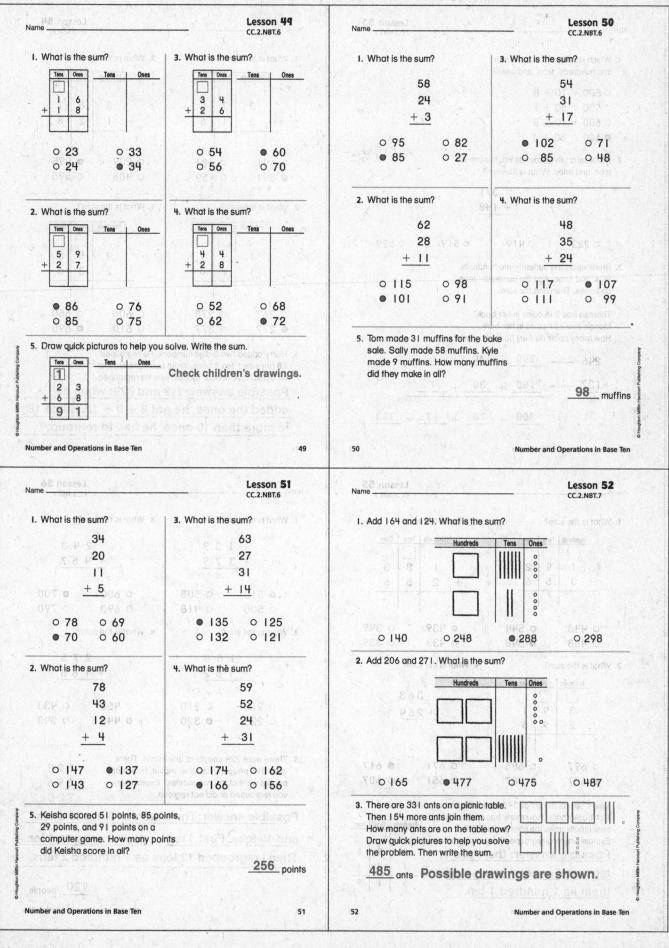

Lesson 49
CC.2.NBT.6

Name _____

1. What is the sum?

	Tens	Ones		Tens	Ones
	☐				
	1	6			
+	1	8			

○ 23   ○ 33
○ 24   ● 34

2. What is the sum?

	Tens	Ones		Tens	Ones
	☐				
	5	9			
+	2	7			

● 86   ○ 76
○ 85   ○ 75

3. What is the sum?

	Tens	Ones		Tens	Ones
	☐				
	3	4			
+	2	6			

○ 54   ● 60
○ 56   ○ 70

4. What is the sum?

	Tens	Ones		Tens	Ones
	☐				
	4	4			
+	2	8			

○ 52   ○ 68
○ 62   ● 72

5. Draw quick pictures to help you solve. Write the sum.

	Tens	Ones		Tens	Ones
	1				
	2	3			
+	6	8			
	9	1			

Check children's drawings.

Lesson 50
CC.2.NBT.6

Name _____

1. What is the sum?

58
24
+ 3

○ 95   ○ 82
● 85   ○ 27

2. What is the sum?

62
28
+ 11

○ 115   ○ 98
● 101   ○ 91

3. What is the sum?

54
31
+ 17

● 102   ○ 71
○ 85   ○ 48

4. What is the sum?

48
35
+ 24

○ 117   ● 107
○ 111   ○ 99

5. Tom made 31 muffins for the bake sale. Sally made 58 muffins. Kyle made 9 muffins. How many muffins did they make in all?

_____98_____ muffins

Lesson 51
CC.2.NBT.6

Name _____

1. What is the sum?

34
20
11
+ 5

○ 78   ○ 69
● 70   ○ 60

2. What is the sum?

78
43
12
+ 4

○ 147   ● 137
○ 143   ○ 127

3. What is the sum?

63
27
31
+ 14

● 135   ○ 125
○ 132   ○ 121

4. What is the sum?

59
52
24
+ 31

○ 174   ○ 162
● 166   ○ 156

5. Keisha scored 51 points, 85 points, 29 points, and 91 points on a computer game. How many points did Keisha score in all?

_____256_____ points

Lesson 52
CC.2.NBT.7

Name _____

1. Add 164 and 124. What is the sum?

Hundreds	Tens	Ones
☐	||||	○○○○
☐	||	○○○○

○ 140   ○ 248
● 288   ○ 298

2. Add 206 and 271. What is the sum?

Hundreds	Tens	Ones
☐ ☐		○○○○○○
☐ ☐	||||||||	○

○ 165   ● 477
○ 475   ○ 487

3. There are 331 ants on a picnic table. Then 154 more ants join them. How many ants are on the table now? Draw quick pictures to help you solve the problem. Then write the sum.

_____485_____ ants **Possible drawings are shown.**

Answer Key

Lesson 53
CC.2.NBT.7

1. Which shows 681 broken apart into hundreds, tens, and ones?

   ○ 500 + 10 + 8
   ○ 500 + 80 + 1
   ○ 600 + 10 + 8
   ● 600 + 80 + 1

2. Break apart the addends into hundreds, tens, and ones. What is the sum?

   $$\begin{array}{r} 371 \\ + 148 \\ \hline \end{array}$$

   ○ 223   ○ 419   ● 519   ○ 529

3. Break apart the addends into hundreds, tens, and ones. Add the hundreds, tens, and ones. Then find the sum.

   Theresa has 246 coins in her bank.
   Maggie has 137 coins in her bank.
   How many coins do they have altogether?

   246 ⟶ 200 + 40 + 6
   +137 ⟶ 100 + 30 + 7
   _____
   300 + 70 + 13 = 383

Lesson 54
CC.2.NBT.7

1. What is the sum?

Hundreds	Tens	Ones
	☐	
3	7	5
+ 2	1	6

   ○ 691   ○ 581
   ● 591   ○ 159

2. What is the sum?

Hundreds	Tens	Ones
	☐	
1	4	9
+ 1	2	8

   ○ 267   ○ 278
   ● 277   ○ 377

3. What is the sum?

Hundreds	Tens	Ones
	☐	
3	6	7
+ 1	2	8

   ○ 239   ● 495
   ○ 485   ○ 595

4. What is the sum?

Hundreds	Tens	Ones
	☐	
4	5	5
+ 2	3	5

   ○ 600   ○ 650
   ○ 610   ● 690

5. Harry added two 3-digit numbers. He regrouped 18 ones as 1 ten 8 ones. Write two numbers that he could have added. Explain why he regrouped.

   Possible answer: 119 and 429; when he added the ones, he got 9 + 9 = 18. Since 18 is more than 10 ones, he had to regroup.

Lesson 55
CC.2.NBT.7

1. What is the sum?

Hundreds	Tens	Ones
☐	☐	
1	9	2
+ 3	5	6

   ○ 448   ○ 544
   ○ 458   ● 548

2. What is the sum?

Hundreds	Tens	Ones
☐	☐	
3	9	1
+ 2	9	6

   ○ 697   ○ 685
   ● 687   ○ 587

3. What is the sum?

Hundreds	Tens	Ones
☐	☐	
1	8	3
+ 2	5	6

   ● 439   ○ 349
   ○ 433   ○ 339

4. What is the sum?

   $$\begin{array}{r} 363 \\ + 254 \\ \hline \end{array}$$

   ○ 671   ● 617
   ○ 651   ○ 607

5. Mike's Sports Shop has 398 baseballs and 121 basketballs. How many baseballs and basketballs does the shop have in all? Explain why you regrouped or did not regroup.

   Possible answer: there are 11 tens, so I needed to regroup them as 1 hundred 1 ten.

Hundreds	Tens	Ones
1	☐	
3	9	8
+ 1	2	1
5	1	9

Lesson 56
CC.2.NBT.7

1. What is the sum?

   $$\begin{array}{r} 139 \\ + 379 \\ \hline \end{array}$$

   ● 518   ○ 508
   ○ 500   ○ 418

2. What is the sum?

   $$\begin{array}{r} 158 \\ + 162 \\ \hline \end{array}$$

   ○ 210   ○ 310
   ○ 220   ● 320

3. What is the sum?

   $$\begin{array}{r} 243 \\ + 457 \\ \hline \end{array}$$

   ○ 600   ● 700
   ○ 690   ○ 790

4. What is the sum?

   $$\begin{array}{r} 275 \\ + 168 \\ \hline \end{array}$$

   ○ 453   ○ 433
   ● 443   ○ 343

5. There were 324 people at one movie. There were 396 people at another movie. How many people were at the two movies? Explain why you regrouped or did not regroup.

   $$\begin{array}{r} 1\,1 \\ 324 \\ + 396 \\ \hline 720 \end{array}$$

   Possible answer: There were at least 10 ones and 10 tens. First, I regrouped 10 ones as 1 ten. Then I regrouped 12 tens as 1 hundred 2 tens.

   720 people

I. There were 487 cars in a parking lot. Then 156 cars left. How many cars are in the parking lot now?

○ 231   ○ 321   ● 331   ○ 336

2. Helen counted 381 leaves on her porch. There were 129 red leaves. How many leaves were not red?

○ 262   ● 252   ○ 250   ○ 249

3. There were 614 boxes at a post office. Then people took 280 boxes home. How many boxes are still at the post office?

○ 434   ○ 420   ○ 344   ● 334

4. Michael collected 525 bottle caps. His sister collected 413 bottle caps. How many more bottle caps did Michael collect than his sister? Draw a quick picture to help you solve the problem. Then write your answer.

Possible drawing:

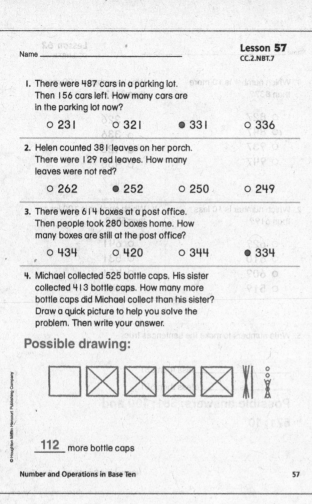

__112__ more bottle caps

I. What is the difference?

Hundreds	Tens	Ones
	☐	☐
7	9	5
− 5	3	7

○ 257   ○ 267
● 258   ○ 268

2. What is the difference?

Hundreds	Tens	Ones
	☐	☐
5	5	7
− 4	1	9

● 138   ○ 148
○ 142   ○ 156

3. Mr. Hansen needs to subtract 145 from 783. Should he regroup? Explain why or why not. Then find the difference.

Yes; Possible answer: He should regroup because there are not enough ones in 783 to subtract 5 ones. He can regroup 1 ten as 10 ones in 783 so there will be 7 tens and 13 ones. Then 13 ones − 5 ones = 8 ones. The difference is 638.

I. What is the difference?

$$\begin{array}{r} 8\ 4\ 7 \\ -\ 3\ 9\ 2 \end{array}$$

○ 559   ○ 539
○ 555   ● 455

2. What is the difference?

$$\begin{array}{r} 4\ 1\ 3 \\ -\ 1\ 5\ 2 \end{array}$$

● 261   ○ 345
○ 341   ○ 565

3. What is the difference?

$$\begin{array}{r} 5\ 4\ 8 \\ -\ 2\ 7\ 6 \end{array}$$

○ 262   ○ 372
● 272   ○ 374

4. What is the difference?

$$\begin{array}{r} 9\ 2\ 4 \\ -\ 4\ 6\ 0 \end{array}$$

○ 584   ● 464
○ 544   ○ 440

5. Sally wants to subtract 461 from 629. Should she regroup? Explain. Then find the difference.

Yes; Possible explanation: There are not enough tens in 629 to subtract 6 tens. Sally should regroup 1 hundred as 10 tens so there will be 5 hundreds and 12 tens. The difference is 168.

I. What is the difference?

$$\begin{array}{r} 7\ 2\ 5 \\ -\ 2\ 8\ 4 \end{array}$$

● 441   ○ 541
○ 449   ○ 545

2. What is the difference?

$$\begin{array}{r} 5\ 6\ 1 \\ -\ 1\ 9\ 3 \end{array}$$

○ 358   ○ 458
● 368   ○ 468

3. What is the difference?

$$\begin{array}{r} 8\ 5\ 2 \\ -\ 6\ 7\ 6 \end{array}$$

○ 276   ● 176
○ 186   ○ 174

4. What is the difference?

$$\begin{array}{r} 6\ 3\ 7 \\ -\ 4\ 5\ 8 \end{array}$$

○ 175   ○ 189
● 179   ○ 271

5. Subtract 189 from 445. Explain how to find the difference. Include regrouping if needed.

$$\begin{array}{r} \overset{3\ \ 13\ 15}{\cancel{4}\ \cancel{4}\ \cancel{5}} \\ -\ 1\ 8\ 9 \\ \hline 2\ 5\ 6 \end{array}$$

Possible answer: I regrouped 1 ten as 10 ones. Then I could subtract 9 ones from 15 ones. I regrouped 1 hundred as 10 tens. Then I could subtract 8 tens from 13 tens.

Answer Key

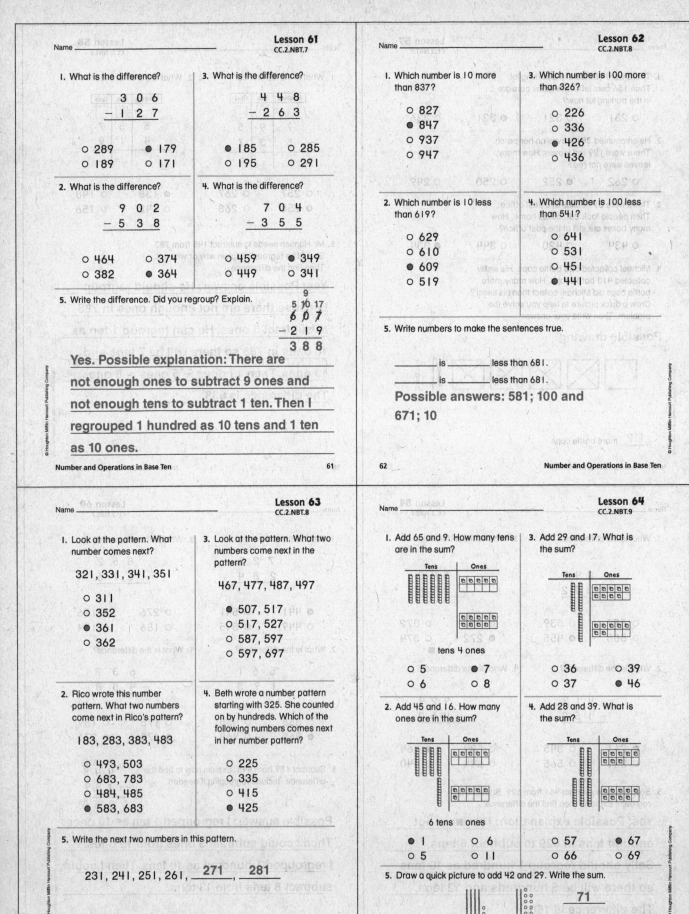

1. What is the difference?

$$\begin{array}{r} 3\ 0\ 6 \\ -\ 1\ 2\ 7 \\ \hline \end{array}$$

○ 289   ● 179
○ 189   ○ 171

2. What is the difference?

$$\begin{array}{r} 9\ 0\ 2 \\ -\ 5\ 3\ 8 \\ \hline \end{array}$$

○ 464   ○ 374
○ 382   ● 364

3. What is the difference?

$$\begin{array}{r} 4\ 4\ 8 \\ -\ 2\ 6\ 3 \\ \hline \end{array}$$

● 185   ○ 285
○ 195   ○ 291

4. What is the difference?

$$\begin{array}{r} 7\ 0\ 4 \\ -\ 3\ 5\ 5 \\ \hline \end{array}$$

○ 459   ● 349
○ 449   ○ 341

5. Write the difference. Did you regroup? Explain.

$$\begin{array}{r} \overset{5}{6}\ \overset{\cancel{10}}{\cancel{0}}\ \overset{17}{\cancel{7}} \\ -\ 2\ 1\ 9 \\ \hline 3\ 8\ 8 \end{array}$$

**Yes. Possible explanation: There are
not enough ones to subtract 9 ones and
not enough tens to subtract 1 ten. Then I
regrouped 1 hundred as 10 tens and 1 ten
as 10 ones.**

1. Which number is 10 more
than 837?

○ 827
● 847
○ 937
○ 947

2. Which number is 10 less
than 619?

○ 629
○ 610
● 609
○ 519

3. Which number is 100 more
than 326?

○ 226
○ 336
● 426
○ 436

4. Which number is 100 less
than 541?

○ 641
○ 531
○ 451
● 441

5. Write numbers to make the sentences true.

_____ is _____ less than 681.
_____ is _____ less than 681.

**Possible answers: 581; 100 and
671; 10**

1. Look at the pattern. What
number comes next?

321, 331, 341, 351

○ 311
○ 352
● 361
○ 362

2. Rico wrote this number
pattern. What two numbers
come next in Rico's pattern?

183, 283, 383, 483

○ 493, 503
○ 683, 783
○ 484, 485
● 583, 683

3. Look at the pattern. What two
numbers come next in the
pattern?

467, 477, 487, 497

● 507, 517
○ 517, 527
○ 587, 597
○ 597, 697

4. Beth wrote a number pattern
starting with 325. She counted
on by hundreds. Which of the
following numbers comes next
in her number pattern?

○ 225
○ 335
○ 415
● 425

5. Write the next two numbers in this pattern.

231, 241, 251, 261, __271__, __281__

1. Add 65 and 9. How many tens
are in the sum?

Tens	Ones

tens 4 ones

○ 5   ● 7
○ 6   ○ 8

2. Add 45 and 16. How many
ones are in the sum?

Tens	Ones

6 tens ones

● 1   ○ 6
○ 5   ○ 11

3. Add 29 and 17. What is
the sum?

Tens	Ones

○ 36   ○ 39
○ 37   ● 46

4. Add 28 and 39. What is
the sum?

Tens	Ones

○ 57   ● 67
○ 66   ○ 69

5. Draw a quick picture to add 42 and 29. Write the sum.

__71__

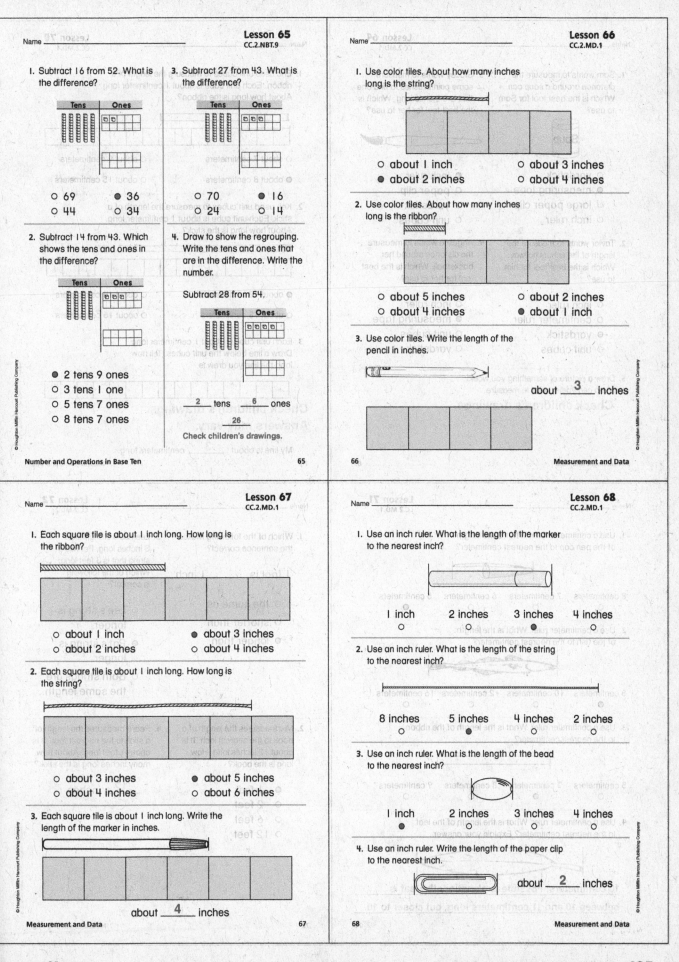

Lesson 65
CC.2.NBT.9

Name _____

1. Subtract 16 from 52. What is the difference?

Tens	Ones

○ 69 ● 36
○ 44 ○ 34

2. Subtract 14 from 43. Which shows the tens and ones in the difference?

Tens	Ones

● 2 tens 9 ones
○ 3 tens 1 one
○ 5 tens 7 ones
○ 8 tens 7 ones

3. Subtract 27 from 43. What is the difference?

Tens	Ones

○ 70 ● 16
○ 24 ○ 14

4. Draw to show the regrouping. Write the tens and ones that are in the difference. Write the number.

Subtract 28 from 54.

Tens	Ones

__2__ tens __6__ ones

__26__

Check children's drawings.

Number and Operations in Base Ten   65

Lesson 66
CC.2.MD.1

Name _____

1. Use color tiles. About how many inches long is the string?

○ about 1 inch   ○ about 3 inches
● about 2 inches   ○ about 4 inches

2. Use color tiles. About how many inches long is the ribbon?

○ about 5 inches   ○ about 2 inches
○ about 4 inches   ● about 1 inch

3. Use color tiles. Write the length of the pencil in inches.

about __3__ inches

66   Measurement and Data

Lesson 67
CC.2.MD.1

Name _____

1. Each square tile is about 1 inch long. How long is the ribbon?

○ about 1 inch   ● about 3 inches
○ about 2 inches   ○ about 4 inches

2. Each square tile is about 1 inch long. How long is the string?

○ about 3 inches   ● about 5 inches
○ about 4 inches   ○ about 6 inches

3. Each square tile is about 1 inch long. Write the length of the marker in inches.

about __4__ inches

Measurement and Data   67

Lesson 68
CC.2.MD.1

Name _____

1. Use an inch ruler. What is the length of the marker to the nearest inch?

1 inch   2 inches   3 inches   4 inches
  ○   ○   ●   ○

2. Use an inch ruler. What is the length of the string to the nearest inch?

8 inches   5 inches   4 inches   2 inches
   ○   ●   ○   ○

3. Use an inch ruler. What is the length of the bead to the nearest inch?

1 inch   2 inches   3 inches   4 inches
  ●   ○   ○   ○

4. Use an inch ruler. Write the length of the paper clip to the nearest inch.

about __2__ inches

68   Measurement and Data

Lesson 69
CC.2.MD.1

Name _____

1. Sam wants to measure the distance around a soup can. Which is the best tool for Sam to use?

Soup

- ○ yardstick
- ● measuring tape
- ○ large paper clip
- ○ inch ruler

2. Taylor wants to measure the length of the school hallway. Which is the best tool for him to use?

- ○ inch ruler
- ○ centimeter ruler
- ● yardstick
- ○ unit cubes

3. Stacey wants to measure some paintbrushes to find one that is 6 inches long. Which is the best tool for her to use?

- ● inch ruler
- ○ paper clip
- ○ yardstick
- ○ unit cubes

4. Angelina wants to measure the distance around her basketball. Which is the best tool for her to use?

- ○ inch ruler
- ● measuring tape
- ○ unit cubes
- ○ yardstick

5. Draw a picture of something you would use a centimeter ruler to measure.

Check children's drawings.

Measurement and Data

69

Lesson 70
CC.2.MD.1

Name _____

1. Eric used unit cubes to measure the length of a ribbon. Each unit cube is about 1 centimeter long. About how long is the ribbon?

- ○ about 7 centimeters
- ● about 8 centimeters
- ○ about 9 centimeters
- ○ about 15 centimeters

2. Ken used unit cubes to measure the length of a stick. Each unit cube is about 1 centimeter long. About how long is the stick?

- ● about 12 centimeters
- ○ about 13 centimeters
- ○ about 14 centimeters
- ○ about 15 centimeters

3. Each unit cube is about 1 centimeter long. Draw a line below the unit cubes. Tell how long the line you drew is.

Check children's drawings.
Answers may vary.

My line is about ___3___ centimeters long.

70   Measurement and Data

Lesson 71
CC.2.MD.1

Name _____

1. Use a centimeter ruler. What is the length of the pen cap to the nearest centimeter?

8 centimeters   7 centimeters   6 centimeters   5 centimeters
     ○   ○   ○   ●

2. Use a centimeter ruler. What is the length of the fish to the nearest centimeter?

8 centimeters   10 centimeters   12 centimeters   16 centimeters
     ●   ○   ○   ○

3. Use a centimeter ruler. What is the length of the ribbon to the nearest centimeter?

5 centimeters   7 centimeters   8 centimeters   9 centimeters
     ○   ●   ○   ○

4. Use a centimeter ruler. What is the length of the leaf to the nearest centimeter? Explain your answer.

10 centimeters; Possible explanation: the leaf is
between 10 and 11 centimeters long, but closer to 10.

Measurement and Data

71

Lesson 72
CC.2.MD.2

Name _____

1. Which of the following makes the sentence correct?

I foot is _____ I inch.

- ○ the same as
- ○ shorter than
- ● longer than

2. Mia measures the length of a book to the nearest inch. It is about 12 inches long. How long is the book?

- ● 1 foot
- ○ 2 feet
- ○ 6 feet
- ○ 12 feet

3. Lee has a string that is 3 inches long. Pat has a string that is 3 feet long. Which of the following is correct?

- ○ Lee's string is longer.
- ● Pat's string is longer.
- ○ Both strings are the same length.

4. Pedro measures the length of a stick to the nearest foot. It is about 1 foot long. About how many inches long is the stick?

___12___ inches

72   Measurement and Data

126

Answer Ke

Lesson 73
CC.2.MD.2

Name _____

1. Which makes the sentence correct?

I centimeter is _____ I meter.

○ the same as
● shorter than
○ longer than

2. Tina measures the length of a table to the nearest meter. It is about I meter long. About how many centimeters long is the table?

○ I centimeter
○ 5 centimeters
○ 10 centimeters
● 100 centimeters

3. Which is the best choice for the length of a real bookshelf?

○ I centimeter   ○ 10 centimeters   ● I meter   ○ 10 meters

4. Would you measure the length of a real car in meters or centimeters? Explain why.

Meters; Possible explanation: centimeters are smaller than meters. It would be faster to count the number of meters.

Lesson 74
CC.2.MD.3

Name _____

1. Lily has some beads that are I inch long each. She wants to put them on a string.

Which is the best estimate for the length of the string?

5 inches   3 inches   2 inches   I inch
   ●   ○   ○   ○

2. Leo has some beads that are I inch long each. He wants to put them on a string.

Which is the best estimate for the length of the string?

I inch   2 inches   3 inches   4 inches
  ○   ●   ○   ○

3. Ann has some beads that are I inch long each. She wants to put them on a string.

Circle the best estimate for the length of the string.

10 inches   5 inches   ⟨3 inches⟩   I inch

Lesson 75
CC.2.MD.3

Name _____

1. Which is the best estimate of the length of a real kitchen table?

○ I foot
● 4 feet
○ 12 feet
○ 20 feet

3. Which is the best estimate of the length of a real baseball bat?

○ 10 feet
○ 7 feet
● 3 feet
○ I foot

2. Which is the best estimate of the length of a real folder?

○ 10 feet
○ 5 feet
○ 3 feet
● I foot

4. Write the best estimate of the length of a real bathtub.

__5__ feet

Lesson 76
CC.2.MD.3

Name _____

1. The length of the string is about 3 centimeters.

Which is the best estimate for the length of the crayon?

I centimeter   2 centimeters   4 centimeters   7 centimeters
    ○   ○   ○   ●

2. The pencil is about 8 centimeters long.

Which is the best estimate for the length of the ribbon?

I centimeter   4 centimeters   9 centimeters   12 centimeters
    ○   ●   ○   ○

3. The straw is about 10 centimeters long. Estimate the length of the paper clip. Explain how you estimated the length.

Possible answer: The paper clip is 5 centimeters long; the straw is 10 centimeters long, and the paper clip seems to be half that size.

Name _____

1. Which is the best estimate for the width of a real stove?

○ about 4 meters   ○ about 2 meters
○ about 3 meters   ● about 1 meter

2. Which is the best estimate for the length of a real bus?

○ about 3 meters   ○ about 6 meters
○ about 4 meters   ● about 12 meters

3. Think about a room in your home. How would you estimate its length in meters?

Possible answer: I would count how many steps I take to walk a meter. Then I would walk across the room and count my steps in groups using that number. The number of groups is the length of the room in meters.

Measurement and Data   77

Name _____

1. Measure the length of each object. How much longer is the celery than the carrot?

1 centimeter   3 centimeters   4 centimeters   7 centimeters
○   ○   ○   ●

2. Which number sentence can be used to find how much longer the ribbon is than the paper clip?

9 centimeters

5 centimeters

○ 9 + 5 = 14   ● 9 − 5 = 4
○ 9 + 4 = 13   ○ 5 − 4 = 1

3. Write a problem about measures. Then subtract.

Check children's work.

_____ is _____ centimeters long.

_____ is _____ centimeters long.

What is the difference in the lengths?

_____

_____

78   Measurement and Data

Name _____

1. Mr. Owen has a board that is 17 inches long. Then he cuts 8 inches off the board. How long is the board now?

9 inches   11 inches   17 inches   20 inches
●   ○   ○   ○

2. Juan has a cube train that is 13 inches long. He removes 5 inches of the cube train. How long is the cube train now?

18 inches   13 inches   8 inches   7 inches
○   ○   ●   ○

3. Meg has a ribbon that is 9 inches long and another ribbon that is 12 inches long. How many inches of ribbon does Meg have in all?

21 inches

Measurement and Data   79

Name _____

1. Karen has a toy car that is 9 centimeters long. She has a toy truck that is 14 centimeters long. She puts them end-to-end. How long are the car and truck together?

18 centimeters   20 centimeters   23 centimeters   25 centimeters
○   ○   ●   ○

2. Matt had a fruit roll that was 13 centimeters long. Then he ate 7 centimeters of the fruit roll. How long is the fruit roll now?

5 centimeters   6 centimeters   8 centimeters   10 centimeters
○   ●   ○   ○

3. Amy drew this diagram to show a problem about lengths in centimeters.

Write a problem that Amy might be trying to solve. Solve the problem.

Possible answer: Amy has a stamp that is 4 centimeters long and a stamp that is 5 centimeters long. She puts them end-to-end. How long are they together?

9 centimeters

80   Measurement and Data

Answer Ke

Lesson 81
CC.2.MD.7

1. Petra's soccer practice starts at 5:00. Which clock shows this time?

○   ●   ○   ○

2. Lee leaves school at 2:30. Which clock shows this time?

○   ●   ○   ○

3. Yolanda leaves for school when the hour hand points halfway between the 7 and 8, and the minute hand points to the 6. What time does Yolanda leave for school? Show the time on both clocks.

     7:30

Measurement and Data   81

Lesson 82
CC.2.MD.7

1. What is the time on the clock? | 2. What is the time on the clock?

○ 3:40   ○ 3:15
● 3:50   ○ 3:00
○ 4:10   ○ 12:10
○ 10:20   ● 12:15

3. Greg went to bed when the hour hand pointed between the 9 and the 10, and the minute hand pointed to the 9. What time did Greg go to bed? Show the time on both clocks.

     9:45

82   Measurement and Data

Lesson 83
CC.2.MD.7

1. Which clock shows half past 7?

○   ○   ○   ●

2. Which clock shows ten minutes after 2?

○   ●   ○   ○

3. Terry's mother looked at a clock. "It's half past 8," she said. "We have to go!" What time did the clock show? Show the time on both clocks. Then write the time another way.

      8:30

Possible answer: 30 minutes after 8

Measurement and Data   83

Lesson 84
CC.2.MD.7

1. Rhonda saw a movie last night. The clock shows when the movie ended.

   9:35

What time did the movie end?
● 9:35 P.M.
○ 9:45 P.M.
○ 9:25 A.M.
○ 9:35 A.M.

2. Keisha has a math test today. The clock shows when the test starts.

   11:10

What time does the test start?
○ 11:10 P.M.
○ 11:20 P.M.
○ 11:05 A.M.
● 11:10 A.M.

3. Write the times you usually eat breakfast, lunch, and dinner.

Breakfast   7:30 A.M.
Lunch   12:15 P.M.   **Possible answers are given.**
Dinner   8:00 P.M.

84   Measurement and Data

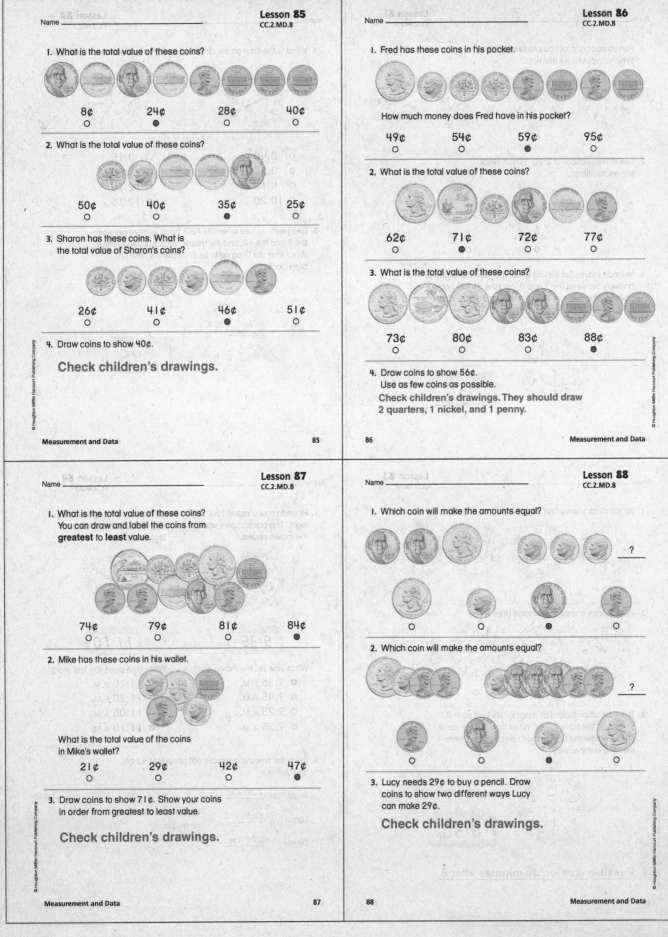

Lesson 85
CC.2.MD.8

Name _____

1. What is the total value of these coins?

8¢ ○   24¢ ●   28¢ ○   40¢ ○

2. What is the total value of these coins?

50¢ ○   40¢ ○   35¢ ●   25¢ ○

3. Sharon has these coins. What is the total value of Sharon's coins?

26¢ ○   41¢ ○   46¢ ●   51¢ ○

4. Draw coins to show 40¢.

Check children's drawings.

Measurement and Data   85

Lesson 86
CC.2.MD.8

Name _____

1. Fred has these coins in his pocket.

How much money does Fred have in his pocket?

49¢ ○   54¢ ○   59¢ ●   95¢ ○

2. What is the total value of these coins?

62¢ ○   71¢ ●   72¢ ○   77¢ ○

3. What is the total value of these coins?

73¢ ○   80¢ ○   83¢ ○   88¢ ●

4. Draw coins to show 56¢.
   Use as few coins as possible.
   **Check children's drawings. They should draw
   2 quarters, 1 nickel, and 1 penny.**

86   Measurement and Data

Lesson 87
CC.2.MD.8

Name _____

1. What is the total value of these coins?
   You can draw and label the coins from **greatest** to **least** value.

74¢ ○   79¢ ○   81¢ ○   84¢ ●

2. Mike has these coins in his wallet.

What is the total value of the coins in Mike's wallet?

21¢ ○   29¢ ○   42¢ ○   47¢ ●

3. Draw coins to show 71¢. Show your coins in order from greatest to least value.

Check children's drawings.

Measurement and Data   87

Lesson 88
CC.2.MD.8

Name _____

1. Which coin will make the amounts equal?

?

○   ○   ●   ○

2. Which coin will make the amounts equal?

?

○   ○   ●   ○

3. Lucy needs 29¢ to buy a pencil. Draw coins to show two different ways Lucy can make 29¢.

Check children's drawings.

88   Measurement and Data

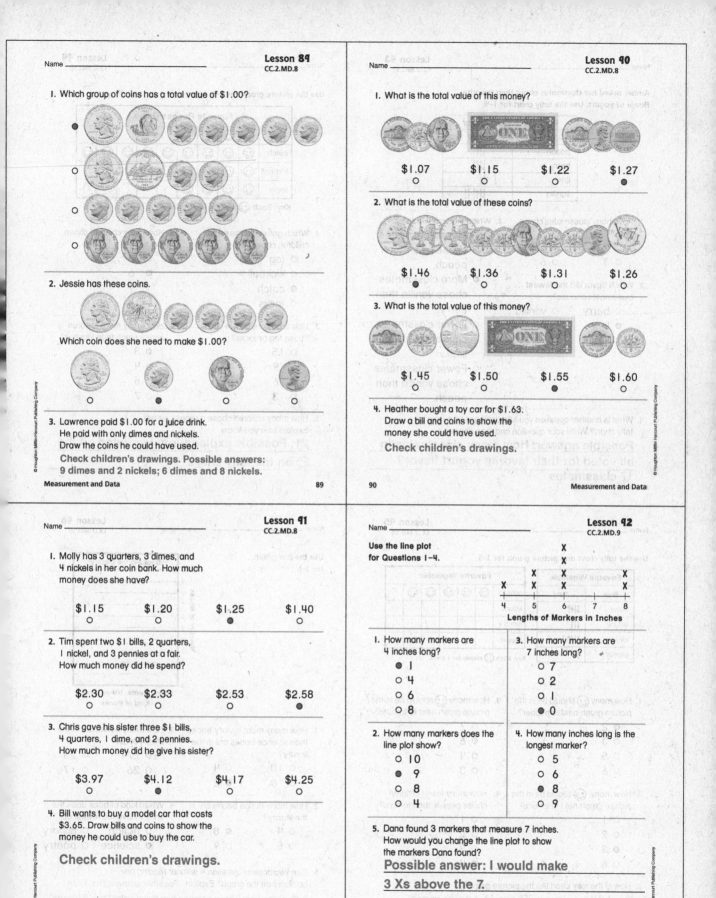

Lesson 89
CC.2.MD.8

Name _____

1. Which group of coins has a total value of $1.00?

2. Jessie has these coins.

Which coin does she need to make $1.00?

○   ●   ○   ○

3. Lawrence paid $1.00 for a juice drink.
He paid with only dimes and nickels.
Draw the coins he could have used.

Check children's drawings. Possible answers:
9 dimes and 2 nickels; 6 dimes and 8 nickels.

Measurement and Data   89

Lesson 90
CC.2.MD.8

Name _____

1. What is the total value of this money?

$1.07 $1.15 $1.22 $1.27
○   ○   ○   ●

2. What is the total value of these coins?

$1.46 $1.36 $1.31 $1.26
○   ○   ●   ○

3. What is the total value of this money?

$1.45 $1.50 $1.55 $1.60
○   ○   ●   ○

4. Heather bought a toy car for $1.63.
Draw a bill and coins to show the
money she could have used.

Check children's drawings.

90   Measurement and Data

Lesson 91
CC.2.MD.8

Name _____

1. Molly has 3 quarters, 3 dimes, and
4 nickels in her coin bank. How much
money does she have?

$1.15 $1.20 $1.25 $1.40
○   ○   ●   ○

2. Tim spent two $1 bills, 2 quarters,
1 nickel, and 3 pennies at a fair.
How much money did he spend?

$2.30 $2.33 $2.53 $2.58
○   ○   ○   ●

3. Chris gave his sister three $1 bills,
4 quarters, 1 dime, and 2 pennies.
How much money did he give his sister?

$3.97 $4.12 $4.17 $4.25
○   ●   ○   ○

4. Bill wants to buy a model car that costs
$3.65. Draw bills and coins to show the
money he could use to buy the car.

Check children's drawings.

Measurement and Data   91

Lesson 92
CC.2.MD.9

Name _____

Use the line plot
for Questions 1–4.

Lengths of Markers in Inches

1. How many markers are
4 inches long?

● 1
○ 4
○ 6
○ 8

2. How many markers does the
line plot show?

○ 10
● 9
○ 8
○ 4

3. How many markers are
7 inches long?

○ 7
○ 2
○ 1
● 0

4. How many inches long is the
longest marker?

○ 5
○ 6
● 8
○ 9

5. Dana found 3 markers that measure 7 inches.
How would you change the line plot to show
the markers Dana found?

Possible answer: I would make
3 Xs above the 7.

92   Measurement and Data

nswer Key   **131**

Amber asked her classmates about their favorite flavor of yogurt. Use the tally chart for 1–4.

Favorite Yogurt Flavor	
Yogurt	Tally
peach	III
berry	ШH
lime	II
vanilla	ШH II

1. How many classmates chose berry?
   ○ 2   ● 5
   ○ 3   ○ 6

2. Which flavor did the **fewest** classmates choose?
   ○ berry   ○ vanilla
   ● lime   ○ peach

3. Which statement is true?
   ○ More classmates chose lime than peach.
   ● More classmates chose vanilla than berry.
   ○ Fewer classmates chose vanilla than lime.
   ○ Fewer classmates chose vanilla than peach.

4. What is another question you can ask based on the tally chart? Write your question and then answer it.
   Possible answer: How many classmates in all voted for their favorite yogurt flavor? 17 classmates

Use the picture graph for 1–5.

Favorite Recess Game									
tag	☺	☺							
catch	☺	☺	☺	☺	☺	☺	☺	☺	☺
kickball	☺	☺	☺	☺	☺	☺			
jacks	☺	☺	☺	☺					

Key: Each ☺ stands for 1 child.

1. Which game did the **most** children choose?
   ○ tag
   ○ kickball
   ● catch
   ○ jacks

2. How many children in all chose tag or jacks?
   ○ 15
   ○ 9
   ● 6
   ○ 3

3. How many children chose kickball?
   ○ 3
   ● 6
   ○ 9
   ○ 15

4. How many more children chose catch than kickball?
   ● 3
   ○ 4
   ○ 5
   ○ 7

5. How many children chose a recess game? Explain how you know.
   21; Possible explanation: I counted all the ☺ on the tally chart.

Use the tally chart and picture graph for 1–5.

Favorite Vegetable	
Fruit	Tally
carrot	ШH
lettuce	III
tomato	ШH I
pepper	II

Favorite Vegetable					
carrot	☺	☺	☺	☺	☺
lettuce					
tomato					
pepper					

Key: Each ☺ stands for 1 child.

1. How many ☺ should be in the picture graph next to pepper?
   ● 2
   ○ 3
   ○ 5
   ○ 6

2. How many ☺ should be in the picture graph next to lettuce?
   ○ 1
   ○ 2
   ● 3
   ○ 6

3. How many ☺ should be in the picture graph next to tomato?
   ○ 7
   ● 6
   ○ 4
   ○ 3

4. How many fewer children chose pepper than tomato?
   ○ 1
   ○ 2
   ○ 3
   ● 4

5. How is the tally chart like the picture graph?
   Possible answer: There is 1 tally mark or ☺ for each person in each one.

Use the bar graph for 1–5.

Books in the Library

1. How many more history books than science books are in the library?
   ○ 10   ○ 4
   ○ 6   ● 2

2. How many fiction books are in the library?
   ○ 4   ● 8
   ○ 5   ○ 9

3. How many books are in the library in all?
   ● 27   ○ 23
   ○ 26   ○ 17

4. Which kind of book does the library have the fewest of?
   ○ fiction   ○ history
   ● science   ○ poetry

5. Can you answer question 4 without reading any numbers on the graph? Explain. **Possible answer: Yes, I can look at the bars. Since science has the shortest bar, it means that the library has the fewest number of science books.**

Use the information for 1–2.
Jorge is making a bar graph about summer sports.

- 5 children played tennis.
- 4 children played baseball.
- 2 children played basketball.

Summer Sports

Number of Children

tennis   baseball   basketball

1. Which could be the missing label in the bar graph?

- ○ Number of Children
- ● Type of Sport
- ○ Tennis
- ○ Soccer

2. How many more children played tennis than played basketball?

- ○ 1
- ● 3
- ○ 2
- ○ 4

3. Tina is making a bar graph to show the number of notebooks her friends have.

- Lara has 4 notebooks.
- Marta has 3 notebooks.
- John has 1 notebook.

Write labels and draw bars to complete the graph.

Check children's work.

Our Notebooks

Number of Notebooks

Lara   Marta   John
Friends

Use the bar graph for 1–4.

Wins by Smithtown Cougars

Month

May
June
July
August

0 1 2 3 4 5 6 7 8 9 10
Number of Wins

1. How many times did the Cougars win in May?

- ○ 8
- ○ 5
- ○ 4
- ● 2

2. How many more wins did the Cougars have in August than in July?

- ○ 6
- ○ 4
- ● 3
- ○ 2

3. Which of the following describes how the number of wins changed from May to August?

- ● The number of wins increased each month.
- ○ The number of wins decreased each month.
- ○ The number of wins stayed about the same.
- ○ The number of wins in August was 8 more than in May.

4. How many times do you think the Cougars will win in September? Explain.

Possible answer: I think they will win at least 9 times in September because the graph shows that they win more games each month, and they won 8 times in August.

---

1. Which of these shapes is a cube?

○   ○

○   ●

2. Which of these shapes is a sphere?

○   ●

○   ○

3. Which of these shapes is a cone?

○   ○

●   ○

4. Which shape does *not* roll?

○   ●

○   ○

5. Draw an X on the shapes that roll.

---

1. How many vertices does a cube have?

- ● 8
- ○ 6
- ○ 4
- ○ 2

2. How many faces does a rectangular prism have?

- ○ 4
- ● 6
- ○ 8
- ○ 12

3. How many edges does a cube have?

- ○ 6
- ○ 8
- ○ 10
- ● 12

4. Which three-dimensional shape could you make with these faces?

- ○ cone
- ○ cube
- ● rectangular prism
- ○ cylinder

5. How many faces, edges, and vertices does a rectangular prism have?

_6_ faces

_12_ edges

_8_ vertices

Answer Key

133

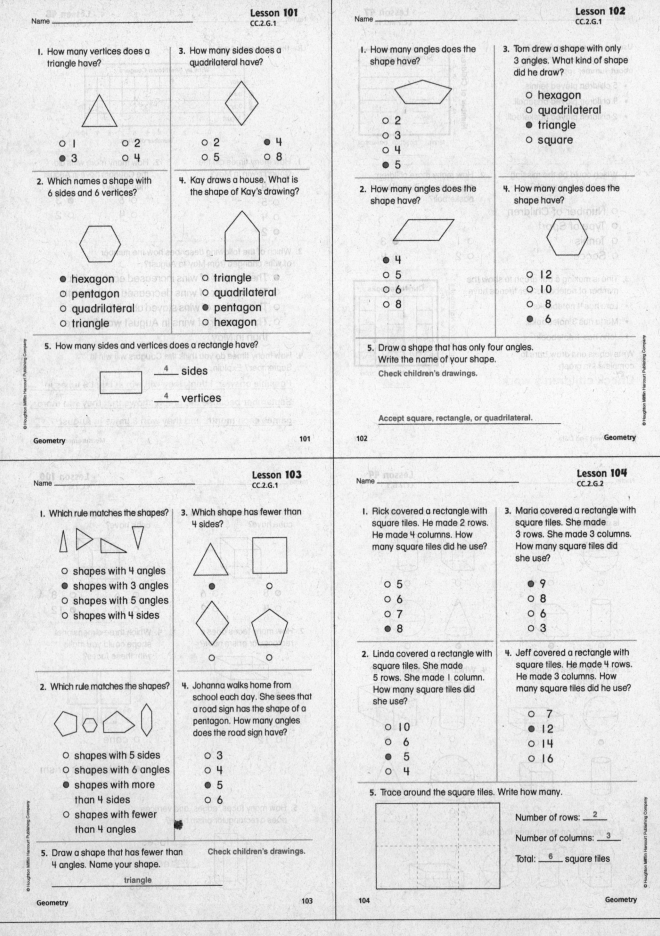

Lesson 101

Name _____

1. How many vertices does a triangle have?

○ 1 ○ 2
● 3 ○ 4

2. Which names a shape with 6 sides and 6 vertices?

● hexagon
○ pentagon
○ quadrilateral
○ triangle

3. How many sides does a quadrilateral have?

○ 2 ● 4
○ 5 ○ 8

4. Kay draws a house. What is the shape of Kay's drawing?

○ triangle
○ quadrilateral
● pentagon
○ hexagon

5. How many sides and vertices does a rectangle have?

__4__ sides
__4__ vertices

Geometry   101

Lesson 102
CC.2.G.1

Name _____

1. How many angles does the shape have?

○ 2
○ 3
○ 4
● 5

2. How many angles does the shape have?

● 4
○ 5
○ 6
○ 8

3. Tom drew a shape with only 3 angles. What kind of shape did he draw?

○ hexagon
○ quadrilateral
● triangle
○ square

4. How many angles does the shape have?

○ 12
○ 10
○ 8
● 6

5. Draw a shape that has only four angles. Write the name of your shape.

Check children's drawings.

Accept square, rectangle, or quadrilateral.

102   Geometry

Lesson 103
CC.2.G.1

Name _____

1. Which rule matches the shapes?

○ shapes with 4 angles
● shapes with 3 angles
○ shapes with 5 angles
○ shapes with 4 sides

2. Which rule matches the shapes?

○ shapes with 5 sides
○ shapes with 6 angles
● shapes with more than 4 sides
○ shapes with fewer than 4 angles

3. Which shape has fewer than 4 sides?

● ○

○ ○

4. Johanna walks home from school each day. She sees that a road sign has the shape of a pentagon. How many angles does the road sign have?

○ 3
○ 4
● 5
○ 6

5. Draw a shape that has fewer than 4 angles. Name your shape.

Check children's drawings.

triangle

Geometry   103

Lesson 104
CC.2.G.2

Name _____

1. Rick covered a rectangle with square tiles. He made 2 rows. He made 4 columns. How many square tiles did he use?

○ 5
○ 6
○ 7
● 8

2. Linda covered a rectangle with square tiles. She made 5 rows. She made 1 column. How many square tiles did she use?

○ 10
○ 6
● 5
○ 4

3. Maria covered a rectangle with square tiles. She made 3 rows. She made 3 columns. How many square tiles did she use?

● 9
○ 8
○ 6
○ 3

4. Jeff covered a rectangle with square tiles. He made 4 rows. He made 3 columns. How many square tiles did he use?

○ 7
● 12
○ 14
○ 16

5. Trace around the square tiles. Write how many.

Number of rows: __2__

Number of columns: __3__

Total: __6__ square tiles

104   Geometry

Answer Key

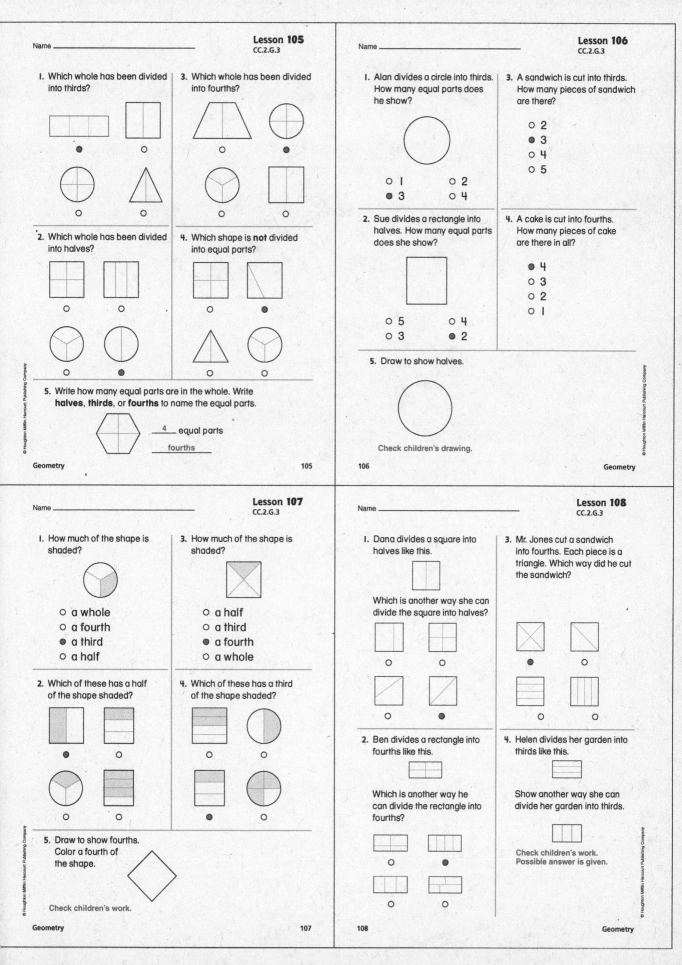

Lesson 105
CC.2.G.3

Name _____

1. Which whole has been divided into thirds?

○ ● ○

○ ○

2. Which whole has been divided into halves?

○ ○

○ ●

3. Which whole has been divided into fourths?

○ ●

○ ○

4. Which shape is **not** divided into equal parts?

○ ●

○ ○

5. Write how many equal parts are in the whole. Write **halves**, **thirds**, or **fourths** to name the equal parts.

_4_ equal parts

fourths

Geometry   105

Lesson 106
CC.2.G.3

Name _____

1. Alan divides a circle into thirds. How many equal parts does he show?

○ 1   ○ 2
● 3   ○ 4

2. Sue divides a rectangle into halves. How many equal parts does she show?

○ 5   ○ 4
○ 3   ● 2

3. A sandwich is cut into thirds. How many pieces of sandwich are there?

○ 2
● 3
○ 4
○ 5

4. A cake is cut into fourths. How many pieces of cake are there in all?

● 4
○ 3
○ 2
○ 1

5. Draw to show halves.

Check children's drawing.

106   Geometry

Lesson 107
CC.2.G.3

Name _____

1. How much of the shape is shaded?

○ a whole
○ a fourth
● a third
○ a half

2. Which of these has a half of the shape shaded?

● ○

○ ○

3. How much of the shape is shaded?

○ a half
○ a third
● a fourth
○ a whole

4. Which of these has a third of the shape shaded?

○ ○

● ○

5. Draw to show fourths. Color a fourth of the shape.

Check children's work.

Geometry   107

Lesson 108
CC.2.G.3

Name _____

1. Dana divides a square into halves like this.

Which is another way she can divide the square into halves?

○ ○

○ ●

2. Ben divides a rectangle into fourths like this.

Which is another way he can divide the rectangle into fourths?

○ ●

○ ○

3. Mr. Jones cut a sandwich into fourths. Each piece is a triangle. Which way did he cut the sandwich?

● ○

○ ○

4. Helen divides her garden into thirds like this.

Show another way she can divide her garden into thirds.

Check children's work. Possible answer is given.

108   Geometry

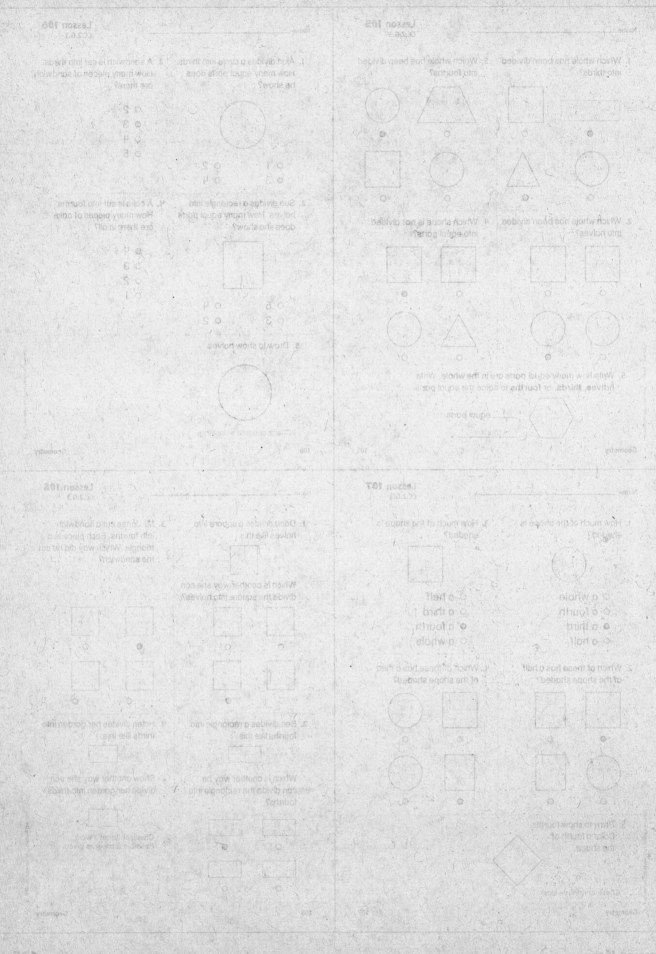